# FINDING MARILYN

## A ROMANCE

# FINDING MARILYN

## A ROMANCE

### BY DAVID CONOVER, THE PHOTOGRAPHER WHO DISCOVERED MARILYN MONROE

Publishers · GROSSET & DUNLAP · New York
A FILMWAYS COMPANY

PHOTO CREDITS: David Conover, pages ii, 6, 8, 11, 18, 23, 39, 40, 41, 42, 47, 79, 81 (below), 82, 200; Sterling's Magazines, Inc., page 2; Jeanne Conover, page 16; United Press International, pages 26, 64, 75, 86, 87, 88, 90, 105, 109, 110, 115, 120, 124–125, 131, 136, 139, 147, 152, 158, 160, 179, 181; 20th Century-Fox, pages 32, 48, 52–53, 55, 62, 96, 102, 104, 112, 128, 149, 155, 170, 174; Wide World Photos, pages 76, 184; George N. Y. Simpson, pages 80–81, 81 (above); Movie Star News, page 100; Henri Dauman/MAGNUM, page 119; Ernst Haas/MAGNUM, page 141; Inge Morath/MAGNUM, pages 144, 176; Alfred Eisenstaedt, LIFE Magazine, © Time Inc., page 165; Jerry Ohlinger, page 168; Eve Arnold/MAGNUM, page 188.

*To my wife, Barbara—*
*for her help and unflagging good spirits*

# Publisher's Note

*I*t is not often that one has a chance to make a real discovery. The world moves too rapidly these days. So it was a special privilege to meet David Conover, the man who took the very first professional photographs of a young woman who was then known as Norma Jean Dougherty. It is even more special to be able to share the private thoughts of this man who so very long ago found the "adorable waif" on a production line at a defense plant in wartime Los Angeles. And how extraordinary that young army photographer David Conover had been sent on his assignment by an Army Air Corps captain who would become President of the United States!

But perhaps the most touching and poignant part of Conover's tale is in his journals, here quoted. They were written over many years of a life lived in the wilderness of a British Columbia island forest. There, far from the encroachment of what we call civilization, remote from the pressures and pastimes of "an ordinary life," Conover thought and dreamed and wrote.

Where does one draw the hard line between dreams and reality? How can one be certain of what has been experienced, imagined, felt? This we do know—that young Conover found her first; that the three of them met, Marilyn, Conover, and the camera. We also know that a few years later David and Marilyn had a joyful reunion on the set of *Gentlemen Prefer Blondes*. It was the sort of thing that press agents dream of, brought about by David's brother, Austin, then a columnist for a Hollywood trade paper.

The contrast is astounding. Conover in his only suit, a baggy tweed befitting a man who emerged only occasionally from the fastness of his island. Marilyn in the sequined gown in which she sang "Diamonds Are a Girl's Best Friend." They stand together off the set and pictures are taken. No one knows what to make of this Conover character, so utterly unHollywood in all his ways. Is it possible that he and Marilyn knew each other? Is it possible that they are friends? Is it possible that they will communicate with each other until Marilyn is so suddenly and mysteriously taken from us?

Every life is a voyage of discovery. Every man's book about himself is a log of that voyage. The publisher invites you to come along on David Conover's voyage. We think what you will discover will add immeasurably to your view of the child-girl innocent erotic we all knew as Marilyn Monroe and how she lived and died.

# *Preface*

My house on Wallace Island, British Columbia, stands on a point above the sea; the island, all green and shimmering, rises up behind it like a gentle mountaintop into the pale blue sky. For more than thirty-five years this world of trees, with the sea thrusting long fingers into it, has been my home and my life.

I have taken root here like the firs. Something of my heart and mind and strength are in this ground and have been all my life. I fell in love with the island as a boy, then I lived here as a pioneer and resort operator, now I am a writer about island life. I told my Robinson Crusoe saga in a trilogy, beginning with *Once Upon an Island;* more island adventures followed in *One Man's Island* and *Sitting on a Salt Spring.*

Since the books I write come out of experiences I have lived, I knew that when the moment came I would write about Marilyn Monroe. For years I had no desire to do so for fear the publicity would disturb or impair my way of life—seclusion was as important to me as attention and fame were to Marilyn. Now that the island chapter of my life has come to a close and I am returning to the shores of society a wealthy man, I feel able to write this book.

A great deal of trash has been written about Marilyn, by people who didn't know her or who didn't know her very well. As a consequence, she has been vastly misunderstood and terribly exploited. Looking back over the seventeen years that I knew Marilyn, I remember her as a bright, extremely bright, woman, with a great sense of humor. She was entirely different from the "dumb blonde" she was made out to be. She was a serious actress, consummate in her ability to establish for all time the American image of the sex goddess. She gave a few remarkable performances, and she made a lot of awful movies nobody cares to remember—but everybody remembers Marilyn. In spite of these films, more than any other star she created her own success. To me her greatest achievement was the creation of Marilyn Monroe.

In many ways, Marilyn and I were opposites, and we dwelt in two different worlds. We were a little more than friends and a little less than lovers, and we found solace, warmth, and joy whenever our lives touched. This is our story.

DAVID CONOVER
*September 1981*

# FINDING MARILYN

## A ROMANCE

AMERICA'S GREATEST MOVIE MAGAZINE
OCT. 20¢
modern screen
DELL MAGAZINE
WHY SHIRLEY TEMPLE CAME BACK
by hedda hopper
I LOVE MARILYN MONROE
by sidney skolsky

*"I was always lonely—that's
why I loved the movies so much."*

August 5, 1962, began like any other day on our island in British
Columbia. The cove glistened in the early morning sunlight like
a Japanese watercolor, and the air held the mingled scent of woods and sea.

I was making breakfast, and as the coffee started to perk I could hear
Jeanne, my wife in those years, stirring in the bedroom. I was turning the
eggs over lightly when the music on the radio was interrupted by the formal
phrase of the Canadian announcer: "Ladies and gentlemen." This would be
serious. He went on: "Marilyn Monroe is dead. Her body was found at three
o'clock this morning in her bedroom by her housekeeper, Mrs. Eunice Murray. An autopsy has been ordered, but the apparent cause of death was an
overdose of sleeping pills. The death of Marilyn Monroe brings to an end
the life of America's reigning sex symbol."

Stunned beyond words, I slumped into a chair. It couldn't be true. Marilyn
dead? No, it was impossible. She had too much to live for. Only ten days
before she had excitedly told me on the phone of several film offers and a
possible Las Vegas engagement.

I got up and went to the window, still unable to accept the terrible news.

I couldn't believe she was dead. I closed my eyes and wept silently while memories of the wonderful girl I once knew and loved as Norma Jean rushed through my mind.

I felt Jeanne's hand on my shoulder. "I'm sorry, David," she said.

I looked at her. "You heard?"

She nodded. "Poor girl. You knew her so well and so much longer than anyone else. It must be a horrible shock." She held out the drink in her hand, a half tumblerful of four-year-old Scotch. "Maybe this will help."

I took several swallows. The announcer was still talking about Marilyn's life and career. The nude calendar . . . Johnny Hyde . . . *Ladies of the Chorus* . . . Joe DiMaggio . . . *Gentlemen Prefer Blondes* . . . Arthur Miller . . . *The Misfits* . . . Clark Gable . . . President Kennedy's birthday party at Madison Square Garden . . .

Finally I snapped off the radio, picked up my glass, and started to leave. "Where are you going?" Jeanne asked, her eyes now as teary as mine.

"To the study," I mumbled.

She looked up into my face. "Listen, darling"—there was concern in her voice—"don't feel guilty. You're not to blame. Whether she killed herself or just took an overdose of pills, it would have happened anyway. Sooner or later."

"Not if I hadn't met her," I blurted.

I closed the study door behind me and took another swallow of Scotch as I stared out the window.

Norma Jean Dougherty. She was only nineteen when I met her, a girl who worked in a defense plant. Separated from her husband, Jim, she was living with an aunt, Ana Lower, in West Los Angeles. Her story—our story—was in my journals. By 1962 I had kept them for some twenty years, and I still keep them. No daily diaries, yet they were and are a record of my life. My thoughts and feelings and beliefs, the highlights of activity that strike me as memorable on a given day, my best recollections of conversations that impress me, the essences of letters from friends and family. I pulled out the volume for 1945, the year I met Norma Jean.

I was an Army photographer then, assigned to the 1st Motion Picture Unit. Our base was familiarly known as Fort Roach, since it was housed in the Hal Roach studio in Culver City, California. The outfit was probably unique in its makeup of personnel, many of whom were stars in uniform; my C.O. was Ronald Reagan.

*May 16*. Guard duty with Kent Smith. Nights very cold and damp and boring. We drank some rum on duty Tues. evg. to keep warm but fell asleep. Was caught by the officer of the day, Lt. Shields. Kent and I spent three days in the guardhouse. Played blackjack—lost 28 dollars. Alan Ladd slipped us in a case of beer—from then on it wasn't too bad.

I kept reading, and remembering.

*June 11*. Huntington Beach today. Photographed new Army recreation center. Met and shot photos of General Doolittle and General Patton. They are so *different*—it's unbelievable.

Two weeks later, on June 25, I celebrated my twenty-sixth birthday ("Too many Zombies! Ugh!").

Then, the entry for June 26, 1945. It begins: "Reagan sent me out to Radioplane Corp., owned by his friend Reginald Denny. Wanted publicity shots of women in war work."

The repercussions of the Zombies were still lingering in my head when Denny welcomed me into his office. He was the dapper, energetic English actor whose face with its waxy black moustache had filled the movie screens in the thirties and who now had turned a model aircraft hobby into the manufacture of radio-controlled miniature planes used by the Army for antiaircraft practice.

"You can't imagine how excited I am," he said, looking at me from behind his broad mahogany desk. "All my life I've played with model aircraft. Now it's paying off." He lit a cigar and puffed ceremoniously. "But don't get me wrong. It's not the bucks. It's that I can help our country. You know, beat the Japs."

I sat there clutching my Speed Graphic, a little overwhelmed by his intensity and dollar-oriented patriotism. Because of my stutter and bifocals, I had always been rather shy and a loner, and not sure how to act with forceful people. "I've been asked," I said finally, "to take morale-boosting shots of pretty girls in defense plants. Do you mind?"

"Not at all." He jumped up and took me into the main assembly room. "Help yourself." He smiled and shook my hand as if it were a dustcloth. "Good luck."

After checking the plant for interesting angles, I moved down the assembly

*On the assembly line at Radioplane Corp., June 26, 1945.*

line, taking shots of the most attractive employees. None was especially out of the ordinary. I came to a girl putting on propellers and raised the camera to my eye. She had curly ash blonde hair and her face was smudged with dirt. I snapped her picture and walked on. Then I stopped, stunned. She was beautiful. Half child, half woman, her eyes held something that touched me and intrigued me.

I retraced my steps. "Say, you don't belong here," I said, immediately feeling foolish for uttering such an unoriginal line. Yet it did seem incongruous to find such a lovely creature in this place.

She looked at me shyly. "Just where do I belong?" she asked softly.

"On a magazine cover."

"Really?"

"Yes, really," I replied, and introduced myself. "And you?"

"I'm Norma Jean Dougherty." She smiled and offered her hand. It was so delicate I had the sensation of grasping a feather. Her eyes scanned my uniform curiously. "What brings the Army here, Private Conover?" Her fragile voice sounded like that of a little girl.

"You," I said.

She giggled. "Hey, you're not serious, are you?" There was a puzzled look in her amazing blue eyes.

I nodded solemnly and explained. Then I asked, "Have you got a sweater?"

"Yes," she said. "I've got one in my locker."

During her lunch break she put it on—a flashy red cashmere that enhanced her astonishing figure delightfully—and from every angle I shot color portraits of her outside the plant in the sparkling sunlight.

Her response to the camera then was amazing. When I had photographed her on the assembly line before her appeal hit me, neither I nor my camera had really concentrated on her, and the result is a static picture of a pretty girl. Now, singled out and with the attention of camera and cameraman focused deliberately on her, she came alive with sure and immediate instinct. I was so excited I could hardly hold the camera steady.

"Am I really photogenic?" she asked.

"I'll tell you as soon as I see the results." But there was no doubt in my mind as I took her phone number and promised to call her when the pictures were ready.

*June 28.* After parade duty I picked up my film at Eastman. The guy asked me who my model was—that she was a *humdinger!* I showed the

7

shots to Norma Jean this evening. She liked them immensely, and I think she was excited about them as much as I. Even her aunt was amazed how beautiful they were. Norma Jean wants to be a movie star. (Seems everybody does these days—ha!) I told her she would have to be a model first, and to think about it.

Aunt Ana was a kindly old lady, very devoted to her niece, and she recognized my concern and regard for Norma Jean. As we all sipped herbal tea together that evening and looked at the photographs, she seemed to sense a turning point in her youthful boarder's life. From that moment on I would have her support.

Seeing the prints and talking to Norma Jean then and over the next few days, I began to develop a plan. By July 1 I was ready to share it with her.

I called for her at Aunt Ana's, but I wanted to talk to Norma Jean alone, so we hopped in the car and went for a drive. On Mulholland Drive, overlooking the glittering lights of Los Angeles, I pulled off the road and turned to her. "Listen," I said, "if you really want to become an actress, will you trust me? Do exactly what I say?"

She considered. "Yes."

"I want you to quit your job at once."

"Why?"

"To take up modeling."

"You mean, right away . . . tomorrow?"

I nodded. "You see, I haven't much time. I'm due to be shipped overseas very soon."

"Oh . . ." she breathed. "That's too bad."

"As soon as you quit"—I leaned over and looked into her eyes—"we're going on a two-week shooting expedition. I'll teach you all I know about modeling. And you'll have a portfolio of prints that will get you work with the top Hollywood photographers. Once you make a few magazine covers, the studios will certainly notice you."

She looked at me in amazement. "You really do believe in me."

"Yes." I smiled. "Very much. But the main thing is you've got to believe in yourself. It's a long, hard, lonely grind to the top."

She glanced at my wedding ring and looked up. "What will your wife say? I mean, being gone two weeks."

"Nothing. I'm often away on assignments."

"Will the Army let you go?" she asked.

"I can arrange it. Ronnie Reagan is my C.O. He's a real brick." (I was showing off a little. A few weeks earlier I'd written in my journal: "Reagan is trying to tighten discipline at Fort Roach. He's stopped all three-day passes. He wants our outfit to march down Hollywood Blvd to the première of his new movie.")

Norma Jean looked doubtful at my show of confidence. "It doesn't sound like the Army to me."

"Fort Roach isn't really the Army." I grinned. "It's the Hal Roach studio in Culver City. It's been converted to turn out training films and combat camera units for the Air Corps. We're called the celluloid commandos."

She laughed. "What a way to fight the war!"

My journal entry about that conversation ends, "She said she'd talk it over with Aunt Ana, and let me know. She seemed very excited about the idea. So am I."

*July 2.* N.J. phoned this a.m. Will be ready to leave Thursday. Great. Will try to see Reagan today. Gosh, she's a sweet girl. I can't wait until we go so I can have her all to myself. Could I be falling in love?

We took off on July 4 in my '37 Ford coupe. (Norma Jean hadn't quit her job—yet—but she had arranged for sick leave.) We headed for the Mojave Desert, planning to go from there to the slopes of Mount Whitney, then drop down into Death Valley and wander back through the lovely ponderosa country around Hemet. That first day we worked at Red Rock Canyon ("Lots of good shots. I think, tho, N.J. is a bit stiff and self-conscious."). When we finished shooting we drove to Bakersfield, and I had an awkward moment.

Didn't quite know how to handle motel "situation." I couldn't afford two rooms. But N.J. was a good sport. She has her bed and I have mine.

But we were both rather shy, and each day of the trip it was a little embarrassing for us both when I signed us in at a motel as a married couple.

Working under the hot desert sun was wearying, and we'd often quit early to look for a motel with a pool and plunge into the cool water. Norma Jean had never learned to swim well, so I began teaching her. After dinner we'd go for a walk, stop at a bar for a drink, and plan the next day's shooting. Each night after dark I'd develop the black and white test shots in the

*Outside the Radioplane Corp. plant, June 26, 1945.*

bathroom, dry them over a portable electric heater, then run them through a small contact printer.

Norma Jean would study every print carefully and ask, "What happened to me here?" Or, "This is awful, where did I go wrong?" And I would tell her. Many times the fault was mine, when I caught her with her eyes shut or my shutter speed wasn't fast enough to freeze her movement. She rarely made the same mistake twice and learned quickly that she photographed best full face, with her lips parted. Each day the percentage of good shots increased.

"You know I can't afford to pay you," she said one night, sounding worried.

"I didn't expect you to."

"You may be wasting your money, you know."

But I could tell by the photographs that I wasn't wasting my money. She had a natural gift for modeling, and she photographed superbly. Even beyond that, there was something special about her, a luminous quality to her face, a fragileness combined with astonishing vibrancy. This girl was going places. I could feel it in my bones.

"You're not only photogenic," I told her, "but someday you're going to be a famous movie star. Believe me."

She was pleased—and scared. "What if I can't act? After all, I've never tried except in those silly school plays. Then I couldn't get the words out."

"Listen," I said, putting my hand on her shoulder, "acting is like any other craft. It can be learned. It's a matter of discipline and practice. Joan Crawford was a chorus girl, Clark Gable was a logger. How far you go depends entirely on your determination. But first of all, young lady, eliminate the word 'can't' from your vocabulary. Then you'll be able to do anything."

She smiled at me. "Shutterbug, you should have been a teacher."

What I really wanted to be was a writer, and I confessed that to her the following night.

"Is that why you keep a journal?" she asked.

I nodded. "It's also a way to keep track of things you don't want to forget."

"Well, the way you handle a camera, a typewriter shouldn't be any problem." She grinned at me.

"I hope so. There should be more than one act in a person's life."

She began to comb her hair in the mirror. "What do you dream about the most?"

"Living on my own island."

"Alone?"

"Oh, no. With Jeanne, of course."

"What would you do?"

"Farm, fish, and write, perhaps. I don't know really."

"Do you have an island in mind?"

"Yes. Wallace Island. Off the coast of British Columbia, where I spent several summers at a boy's camp."

She turned from the mirror. "Hey, you really are a dreamer."

"Aren't we all?"

Each morning we'd shove off early with a picnic lunch and a six-pack of beer and wander down dirt roads until we spotted a brook or a meadow full of wildflowers. Norma Jean was lovely lying among the buttercups, her hair sparkling with flecks of gold, fanned out around her on the mossy ground. She was still lovelier when she emerged from a stream and waded toward the camera, her golden skin glistening and her face aglow with that radiant smile. "Hold it!" I'd shout. "That's it. Don't move." And I'd snap the shutter.

"How did I do?" she always asked with a girlish grin.

I resisted superlatives. "Not bad, really," I'd say.

But neither was she always that good. Sometimes she had a vacuous expression that puzzled me. It was as though for a brief moment she totally lacked an identity. Her face was a void then, waiting for some uniqueness to give it character. Knowing her unsureness, sometimes I would romantically interpret this blank look as reflecting the fear of a young girl on the brink of womanhood; later I suspected that it was a carryover from a difficult childhood. It never came to her face when she was animated, so I made a habit of telling her jokes while I photographed her, or saying silly things: "Think like a soggy doughnut," or, "Pretend you're a pretzel." My funning, however, did not always achieve the desired effect. One time, while posing on a split-rail fence, she began to laugh so hard she toppled off backwards into a thicket of blackberry vines. She was so badly scratched we canceled shooting for the rest of the day.

She was a delightful companion, uncomplicated and always herself: gay, kind, witty, giggly, tender, playful. I loved tramping through the woods with her. I've never seen anyone derive so much pleasure from all living things. She loved the trees, the flowers, the birds; and it gave me great pleasure to point out the different wildlife and tell her about the plants that abounded in the forest. "Jim used to take me on hunting trips," she told me once. "But I hated it. When he shot rabbits I had to close my eyes." She glanced at me.

"Do you like to hunt?"

"Only with this," I said, patting my camera.

She smiled, pleased. "That's good."

One day, after we had spread our blanket on the ground and eaten our tuna sandwiches with gulps of beer, Norma Jean began to tell me about her childhood. "I was terribly shy and stuttered a lot," she said. "I suppose it was because I never felt secure growing up in so many foster homes. To get rid of me my foster parents used to send me to the movies. Sometimes I went four or five times a week. I was always lonely—that's why I loved the movies so much. I could completely forget myself. When I got home I closed the bedroom door and acted out the parts that I saw on the screen. For a twelve-year-old, it was very serious pantomime. I had a crush on every movie star. But my real heartthrob was Clark Gable. He was my idol and hero."

She took a swallow of beer and rolled over on the grass. Her hands under her head, she stared at the sky. "My greatest dream," she said, "is that when I become an actress I'll star opposite him. That would be the top. After that I don't think there'd be much else to live for." She looked at me. "Does that sound crazy?"

"Decidedly." I smiled at her. "Would you like to meet him?"

"Sure. And maybe I could sprout wings and fly."

"Hey, I'm not kidding. Gable is a friend of mine. He was stationed with me at Fort Roach before he was discharged."

"No joking?" She still didn't believe me.

"Honest. I've known him six years now."

She sprang up. "How did you ever meet him? I mean, it must have been before the war."

"It's a long story . . ." I warned.

"If it's about Gable, I could listen forever. Tell me," she begged.

"Well, the first time was in 1939, when my college buddy and I took the old Ford and headed into the desert to explore Baja California."

"You mean, where there are no roads?"

I nodded. "That's what got us in trouble. We were traveling down a riverbed that wasn't as hard and dry as it looked. Before we knew it we were up to our axles in mud."

"What did you do?"

"Started digging. But it was a slow process. We had no shovels. While we were poking away at the mud with sticks this great big Dodge station wagon pulled up on the bank and out stepped Clark Gable and Carole Lombard."

14

"Really?" Norma Jean's eyes beamed.

"Really."

" 'You boys need some help?' Gable asked. We nodded wanly, and he got two shovels. With mud up to his knees, he helped us dig out while Carole stood on the bank and yelled at Pappy—that's what she called him—for getting so filthy dirty."

"Was her language as foul as everyone says?" she asked.

"Umm, yes, I'm afraid so. But it was obvious they were very much in love."

"When was the next time you saw him?" Norma Jean's curiosity about Gable knew no bounds.

"Two years later, when my buddy and I again headed into Baja, looking for a very remote lake high up in the San Pedro Martirs. The going was rough. Half the time the old mining road was either washed out or littered with boulders. Not many people ever reach Laguna Hansen, but guess who was up there?"

"Not Gable and Lombard?"

"Yup. They were camping at the edge of the lake. Gable took one look at us and groaned, 'Not you two again.' And he broke into that sly grin. 'Are you following us, by chance?' Later we learned that the newspapers had reported them missing and a search party had been formed to look for them. They were seldom allowed a moment's privacy."

"When did you see him again?"

"A couple of weeks later. We were invited to his home in Encino for dinner."

"Oh, wow!" she exclaimed. "Did you go?"

"You bet."

"Tell me about it."

I glanced at my watch. "It's getting late. Maybe some other time. We'd better look for a motel."

We were driving through the outskirts of Barstow and neon "no vacancy" signs were popping up everywhere in the dusk. "You think a lot of Gable, don't you?" she asked.

"Yes," I replied, keeping my eyes on the road. "You know why? He takes a genuine interest in people. Little people. He even waves to me when we pass each other on Wilshire Boulevard. He's really a great guy." Fifteen years later, Norma Jean learned this for herself.

She was silent a moment. Then, "Tell me, Shutterbug," she asked, "do

*Private David Conover, U.S.A.*

you really think I can get my picture on a magazine cover?"

"Of course," I said. "You're a natural. If I don't manage it, some other photographer will. But right now you should think about going to modeling school."

"Any one in particular?"

"Yes. Miss Snively's. She runs the Blue Book Model Agency in Hollywood. It's the best."

"How much does it cost?"

When I told her one hundred dollars, I saw the disappointment in her eyes. "But don't you worry," I added quickly, smiling. "There's an old Arabic proverb that says, 'If a goal is fiercely embedded in thy heart, doors shall be opened unto you.'"

*"I won't go in there! I'm not an orphan! I'm not! My mother isn't dead, is she, Aunt Grace? She's not dead!"*

*J*uly 7. This Barstow is hot as Hades. Stayed in the pool until the sun went down and guzzled beer. Norma Jean doesn't like the hard stuff. Prefers the bubbly wine. After a few beers, N.J. told me about her mother—that she was institutionalized, and was afraid her mental condition would be passed on to her.

I didn't know what to say. Since Norma Jean was now living with Aunt Ana and had mentioned many different foster homes—and never her parents—I had simply assumed they were dead.

"I'm sorry," I said. "But that doesn't mean you have anything to worry about. It could be a temporary breakdown, or maybe premature senility."

She stared at me. "But insanity runs in the family. Both Mother's parents died insane. I don't know how far it goes back, or how long it will go forward. I just know I have . . . it's like an omen . . . the awfulest nightmare." She stopped, her eyes wide and startled, as if terrified by the memory. Then she turned her head away. I had never seen a face so lost and lonely and afraid.

"Listen," I said, trying to soothe her fears. "That doesn't mean you'll go

19

crackers. You can inherit blue eyes or blonde hair, but not most illnesses. Besides, all this is on your mother's side. What about your father and his parents?"

"I never knew my father," she replied bluntly.

"You mean he died when you were little?" My own father had died when I was four, so I thought I could understand what she must feel. But I was totally unprepared for what she said next.

"I never knew my father," she repeated, "because I never knew for sure who he was."

"Why?" I was taken aback. "I mean, your mother—she was married, wasn't she?"

Norma Jean looked down. "Mother is very mixed up. She doesn't remember things the same way. Her stories always seem to change. I don't know whether she deliberately lies or just gets confused." Her agitation was increasing now with every word. "It's so depressing. I don't know what to believe."

The sun was going down now, the pool lights came on, and we slowly, silently, went inside. The cool, darkened motel room felt good after the intense heat. I poured two more beers, the last left in the cooler from the day's shooting, and we sat on the couch in the semidark.

I looked at Norma Jean. Her face was pale and taut, her gaze restless. I felt sorry for her. "Look" I began uncertainly, "if it'll make you feel better, tell me more. I'm a good listener."

"You don't mind?" she asked.

"No, not at all."

My stutter had always made it much easier and more satisfactory for me to listen rather than talk. Now, however, I found myself asking questions. "Was your mother always—that way?"

"Yes, ever since I can remember. But I don't really know her. You see, Mother didn't raise me at all. I was brought up in an orphanage, and then in foster homes."

I was stunned. "How much did you see of your mother? Did you ever live with her?"

"I lived with her once for several months. Just one Christmas. That's all." Her voice was flat. "She was really just the woman my foster parents told me to call 'Mama' when she'd visit. She's almost a total stranger to me. So I'm really nothing but an orphan. But oh! how I fought going back to the orphanage!"

20

I nodded. There was nothing to say.

"They had to drag me inside the building," she went on, her eyes very big and her hands pressed tightly together. "I remember screaming, 'I won't go in there! I'm not an orphan! I'm not! My mother isn't dead, is she, Aunt Grace? She's not dead!' But now I don't fight it anymore." She looked up at me. Her voice was cold and tight. "I really *am* an orphan."

I was watching Norma Jean as she talked, and it seemed a miracle to me that she could have survived this sort of upbringing as she had; her very intelligence and freshness, yes, her gentleness, too, were in complete contrast to everything she was describing. I had the feeling she had kept too much bottled up inside her, too much for her own good. Now she was reaching out in her anguish for help—as she would again and again over the years—and I didn't know how to help, or what to say.

I asked about her father. "Didn't your mother tell you about him?"

"Once," she said, "before I went to live with her. She told me my father was her dead husband. But while I lived with her that Christmas she showed me a picture of a different man she said was my father. He looked like Clark Gable, big and manly. In fact, I used to tell my school friends that Clark Gable was my secret father. They never knew whether to believe me or not."

"Didn't you ask her about the different stories?"

She nodded. "Yes, but she denied having told them. She said I was too young and had things all mixed up. And told me that Mortensen, her husband, died two years before I was born."

"Have you ever met the man she said was your father?"

"No"—I thought she was beginning to cry— "but I often dream of finding him, and going to see him or call him. Just to hear his voice, even just to hear him say 'hello' or 'goodbye' or shout 'get out of my life.' Just to know that he's real and not just paper. To know I have two halves." She stared into her glass. "Sometimes I feel incomplete, like only half a person. Like I'm not quite real, and it scares me. But not as much as the nightmare I keep having."

I put my arms around her and I could feel her shoulders trembling a little. "Tell me about it," I said softly.

"No. Maybe later. I've yakked enough about my problems. I don't want to bore you."

"You don't. Really."

She smiled and stood up. "Come on, Shutterbug. Let's go for a swim."

At night, while I developed film, Norma Jean would read. She had brought along a copy of Mary Baker Eddy's *Science and Health* and made a practice of reading it daily. I was curious, and I asked her where she got it.

"Aunt Ana gave it to me," she said, proudly showing me the inscription. It read: "Norma dear, read this book. I do not leave you much except my love, but not even death can diminish that; nor will death ever take me far away from you."

"Your Aunt Ana is quite a woman. I liked her right away."

"She's my very best friend. On Sundays we go to church together. But I don't go to the testimonial services. They're too depressing." She paused. Then, "Do you know anything about Christian Science?"

"A little."

"What do you think of it? I mean, does it make sense to you?"

I thought for a moment. "Religion is a very personal thing. What might be good for you might not be good for me. So it's not for me to say. It's a matter of individual choice."

She grinned at me. "You hedge beautifully."

"I'm a Cancer. They're the master hedgers of the zodiac." I smiled.

"You believe that stuff?"

"From what I've read, a lot of it seems true."

"Hey, there you go again." She giggled. "You never answer a question directly."

"I know." Norma Jean had caught me—I felt a little chagrined. "Cancers seldom do. They feint and dodge and move sideways like a crab. That's why they make such good diplomats."

"Hey, you really dig that stuff."

I admitted that I had studied astrology. "It's fun seeing how people match their birth signs."

She looked at me. "My birthday is June first. Do you think I'm a true Gemini?"

"It's hard to say."

"Oops!" She began to giggle. "You did it again."

I smiled at her. "Okay, let's see if you have these characteristics. You're the sparkler of the zodiac. Lively, witty, and charming."

"Possibly. But I've never thought of myself like that."

"Yet just beneath the glitter, you're restless and a loner. Changeable, sometimes flighty, easily bored but never boring to others. Your sparkle radiates from an inner glow. And like the firefly you need a lot of freedom to keep on glowing."

22

"Hey, that's me." She was laughing.

"You have two or more distinct personalities," I added.

"That's true," she replied excitedly. "Sometimes I feel I'm two totally different people. One an introvert, the other—"

"An extrovert?" I smiled.

"Yes. I think that's why I'm so restless."

"And why you're supremely happy and full of life one moment, then sad, quiet, and withdrawn the next?"

"Yes."

"And often frustrated and discontented?"

"Right."

"Shall I go on?"

"Oh, yes." She was enjoying this.

"Okay. Geminis fall in love easily and often. But a certain detachment marks their relationships. They'd rather have a close friend than a lover."

Norma Jean put her index finger to her lips in a gesture I was beginning to recognize; she often used it when she was puzzled or confused. "That's odd. Why?"

"They're very independent. Friendship requires far less emotional commitment."

Her curious bright blue eyes looked at me. "Do Geminis make good actresses?"

"The best," I said. "Look at Barbara Stanwyck, Rosalind Russell, Gertrude Lawrence, Isadora Duncan. You can go on indefinitely."

"Whoopee!" she cried like a delighted child. "The stars are on my side!"

This was not altogether true. Astrology tells us that Geminis with their split personality are often thereby prevented from achieving their goals, while their adaptability and innate sense of drama enable them to play to perfection every role they adopt because they are masters of deception. It is not uncommon for Geminis to live several lives at the same time.

I smiled at her. "All you have to add is grit and determination."

Later, when we had showered and were ready for bed, Norma Jean looked over at me. "You're only seven years older than me. How come you know so much?"

"Because I'm a slug."

"A slug?"

"A slug in the garden of knowledge. I eat up everything in sight."

But I hadn't fully shared my knowledge with her. I hadn't mentioned that Geminis tend to have difficulty telling the difference between truth and falsehood; they rarely find contentment or happiness in marriage; that they can be critical and sharp-tongued; that they are inclined to be unpunctual, even for important appointments; that they cannot endure either routine or defeat. Except for the tendency to be late, none of these characteristics seemed to fit the lovely, soft-spoken Norma Jean. But later, the Marilyn Monroe the world knew was the classic example of the complete Gemini.

*With Laurence Olivier, July 16, 1956.*

*"I am different. I want to give up
everything to do one thing well. To be
a great actress is more than a dream
or a career. It's my whole mission in life."*

*July 8.* N.J. began to talk about her marriage. She said she wasn't cut out to be a housewife. "Poor Jim. I know I disappointed him. But I wanted more out of life than dishes, ironing, and scrubbing." I said some people weren't cut out for traditional roles, and I wasn't either.

Norma Jean told me she had married Jim Dougherty to stay out of the orphanage. "I was only sixteen. My foster parents were moving East and didn't want to take me. Aunt Ana wasn't able to keep me. And foster homes for teenagers were difficult to find. So it meant going back to the orphanage."

"You must have really dreaded that," I said.

"Dreaded!" she exclaimed "That's hardly the word. It was the end of the world. I felt desperate, panicky and helpless. I wanted to die." The anguish in her voice was reflected in her face.

"Marriage was your only alternative?"

She was at the window, staring at the darkening sky. "Yes," she said.

"Hardly a good basis for marriage," I mumbled, not knowing what else to say.

27

She turned and looked at me. "I didn't think of that then. There wasn't much time. I was desperate. When my foster parents suggested I marry Jim it seemed like a good idea. Fortunately, he thought so too. I was so relieved and grateful."

"You did know him?"

"Oh, yes." Her eyes brightened. "He was the catch of the neighborhood. I had dated him and for a while I had a crush on him. I was so happy not to have to go to the orphanage. And I thought surely I could love someone who would do that for me."

"But it didn't work out that way, did it?"

"No. I hated housework. And he made fun of my attempts at cooking. Besides, I was bored. Poor Jim. I know I disappointed him. I wanted more out of life than dishes, ironing, and scrubbing."

I smiled. "Some people aren't cut out for traditional roles. I don't think I am."

She came over and sat down beside me. Her eyes looked up at me warmly. "I'm glad to hear you say that."

"Why?"

She drew a deep breath. "I've always felt that I am different. I want to give up everything to do one thing well. To be a great actress is more than a dream or a career. It's my whole mission in life." She paused and stared at me. "You don't find that childish, do you?"

"No, not at all," I assured her. "To do anything really well takes complete dedication. A very rare and admirable quality."

"I'm glad you think so." She sighed. "Anyone else would laugh at me. Jim did once. He felt threatened, I guess. But you're so understanding."

Her eyes were somber and thoughtful as I studied her. "It's funny," she continued, looking into her glass, "but I have the feeling—I don't know why—that our meeting wasn't by accident. Do you feel that, too?"

"Definitely. I've felt it all along."

She moved closer to me and her eyes met mine. "Tell me. Do you have a goal? I mean, a mission, too?"

"Yes, I do."

"What?"

"To become a better gardener."

"A gardener!" she exclaimed, mystified.

"Talent scout might be a better word." I smiled at her. "You see, people are my secret garden. I delight in extracting from each person I know all the perfection and beauty they hold."

Her eyes widened. "That's why you've gone out of your way to help me?"

Embarrassed, I nodded. "Probably."

"And work so hard. So hard sometimes I think you forget I'm a woman as well as a model."

"I'm sorry. I didn't mean to . . ."

"That's all right. Skip it." She got up and took off her robe. "Will you turn out the lights? I think I'll hit the sack."

Later, after I got into bed, Norma Jean raised herself up on her elbow in the semidarkness. "Forgive me for what I said. I didn't mean to be unkind. I'm really very grateful."

"That's okay. I do get carried away with my camera. Forget everything else. I'll try to be more considerate."

She threw her head back on the pillow and began to laugh long peals of laughter, as if what I had said made no sense.

"Is anything wrong?" I asked, perplexed.

"No, no," she said. Then she giggled. "Just skip it."

I was trying to think of the reason for her outburst when she said, "I'm curious." She rose again on her elbow. "Have you been helping anyone else?"

"Oh, I've taken a few shots of a girl named Adele Jergens. Very classy dark brunette. She wants to become an actress, too. She could do well. But she doesn't seem to have the tremendous drive you do."

"Anyone else?" she asked.

"Yes, a young hospital orderly who sculpts at night. His figurines and busts were lovely, the work of an extraordinary talent. But he had a problem—how could he sell them? They were too bulky to pack around on a bus."

"What did you do?"

"I told him I'd photograph them. He said no, that he didn't have the money. I said that didn't matter. I told him, 'I've never done this before. It'll be good experience.' "

Norma Jean asked, "Did you?"

I nodded. "With a portfolio of prints, he persuaded bookstores and art supply shops to exhibit his work. My Ford provided the transportation. He was making sales in no time. Then art galleries began to exhibit his work. From the last report, Lowell Grant is on his way towards becoming a world-renowned children's sculptor."

"You do wonders with your camera," she said breathlessly. "I hope you can do the same for me."

"I hope so, too," I said sleepily.

In her fragile voice, she whispered, "Goodnight, Shutterbug."

"Goodnight, beautiful."

*July 10.* 2nd day in Death Valley (Furnace Creek Inn). Shooting in the sand dunes. Very hot and tiring. N.J. is very patient, stands for shot after shot in the blazing sun. She is learning fast that a model must keep her cool. We swim a lot in the pool. N.J. can do about five strokes now before she starts to flounder. I wanted to take a shot of her in the room last night after getting out of the shower but she said *NO.* She said all I think about is my damn camera. What about her? "Do you think I'm made of stone? Don't you find me desirable?" I didn't know what to say I was so embarrassed. I said, of course, you're desirable—I want to put my arms around you all the time. Well, why don't you, she said. We've slept in separate beds for a week. We don't have to. Is there something wrong with me? No, I said, it just wouldn't be right. Why? she asked. I stammered that I would be taking advantage of the situation, that I don't want to. I don't want or need any favors. She broke into laughter and sat on the bed beside me. Shutterbug, you're so funny. When two people are together night after night, no one is doing anybody else a favor. She dropped the big white beach towel around her breasts and put her arms around me and kissed me and whispered, let's do what comes naturally. We did.

The next morning was the first time I saw her get dressed. Our clothes were scattered on the floor. She reached for her blue-striped T-shirt and pulled it on. "Shut your eyes while I get my slacks on," she said, which I did—almost—as she struggled into them. Her shyness now seemed as natural and unaffected as her nakedness in bed. I asked her if she'd pose in the nude. She declined very modestly, saying she might live to be sorry. Several years later, of course, when Tom Kelley took the famous nude calendar photo of her and the publicity helped to boost her career, she had no cause for regret.

While we ate breakfast in the coffee shop, I leaned towards her. "How come you don't wear underthings?" I whispered.

She laughed. "I hate anything that restricts me." She leaned closer. "You don't wear jockeys, do you?" What a girl!

When we were ready to leave, she hopped into the car and settled contentedly in the seat beside me. She was wearing very little makeup and her curly hair was neatly covered by a red bandanna.

"You're looking great," I said as we turned on to the highway.

"I have every reason to." She smiled and kissed me on the cheek. "Where are we going today?"

"Lone Pine. There's an old movie set not too far from town. Mount Whitney's behind it, and it's quite pretty. Did you see *Brigham Young* with Tyrone Power and Linda Darnell?"

"Oh, yes. I loved it."

"Well, we're going to spend the day where they shot the movie. I hope vandals haven't ripped the place apart."

"How did you know about it?"

"I ran across it when I was doing a series of photographs for Standard Oil's 'See the West' campaign."

The *Brigham Young* set was a small, crude pioneer village beneath a range of snowcapped mountains. As we wandered through it, Norma Jean said to me in amazement, "The stores and house are only fronts! They're not buildings at all!"

I laughed. "Now you know what a movie set is like."

"Are they all this way?" she asked.

"Yes. Entirely two-dimensional."

She swung open the door of a saloon and was greeted by miles of rolling countryside. "How disappointing." She turned to me. "It's so false and un-romantic."

"But practical for the moviemaker."

"Where do they shoot the interior scenes?"

"In the studio, using mock rooms, false backgrounds, and props."

"Oh, don't tell me any more. It'll spoil every movie I see."

"Okay," I said, aiming my camera at her. "Suppose we start to work. It's nearly three o'clock."

*With Alex D'Arcy in* How to Marry a Millionaire, *1953.*

*"I could never be a kept woman or marry just for money. I like my independence too well."*

Now that we had become intimate, we felt more relaxed with one another and began to talk more freely. Norma Jean was incapable of saying an unkind word. She seemed completely innocent, unable to see evil in anything. This quality was undoubtedly the result of her belief in Christian Science; later on it would become the basis of her screen image. Walking down the street, I found myself naturally taking the curb side, and I realized I felt a sort of protectiveness towards her.

Norma Jean was easy to be with, easy to appreciate. I liked her bubbly disposition, her frequent musical laugh, her determined stride, her candor, her genuine interest in people, and the zeal she put into her work. I enjoyed her in and out of bed, because there was no meanness, no fussiness in her. No thin upper lip, no pug ill-tempered nose, no deceit or trickiness in her eyes. She was as wholesome and fresh and sweet as an orange blossom. And she had the rare quality of being a good listener.

She was extremely bright, and despite her meager education—she never finished high school—her curious mind was eager for enrichment. I would rarely see a bookstore without dragging Norma Jean inside and plying her with an armful of cheap editions, usually classics that I thought she'd enjoy. I bought her copies of *The Snow Goose* and *Green Mansions* and at night read her my favorite passages while she curled up beside me, her lips parted in a smile of delight. I loved to listen to her reactions to the things we read and saw together, and then I would point out their literary or historical significance. Though I claimed no particular understanding of human nature, especially the female psyche, I was rich in book knowledge. Once, at a quiet roadside restaurant, I put my philosophy in a nutshell. "It isn't how much we know, Sweetheart. It's the quality of what we know that makes us a better person."

"Hey, that's nice." She smiled. "Did you write that in your journal?"

"Probably, because that's the way I feel," I said. Trying not to sound too pedantic, I added, "You see, it's the capacity to enjoy the extraordinary that lifts us above the ordinary. To become somebody, you've got to *be* somebody."

"Wow!" she breathed. "You're a philosopher, too."

I laughed. "No, just a bookworm."

The emphasis of our journey was turning from photography to our pleasure in each other. We were extremely comfortable together and completely open with one another, which made us feel we had known each other for years. We found that we had many interests in common—good music, dancing, movies, the funny papers, the ocean (she could literally smell water a mile or two away)—not to mention the great outdoors. We began to take longer lunch breaks, sometimes well into the afternoon, because as soon as we finished eating we opened our books. We spent more time talking, laughing, having fun.

*July 14.* N.J. has a lively sense of humor. As we drove along looking for a motel tonight she said if you don't speed up we'll get a ticket for parking in the middle of the road. She loves me to read Keats to her, particularly my favorite passages from his letters. I told her I admired his courage. She said why, and I said because he faced both life and death bravely. Nothing stopped the guy. Even while dying of TB he wrote his greatest poetry. A perfect example how moral qualities propel talent to greatness. N.J. asked if this was true of acting. Yes, courage and direction are the cornerstones of art. Particularly in Hollywood where talent is abundant, but full achievement of it is rare. I told her I knew many movie stars, and heard the stories of their lives as I worked with them at Fort Roach. Because of this contact I said that after the war I might be able to get her a screen test, as one of my friends and co-workers at Fort Roach was Leon Shamroy, one of Hollywood's top cameramen. She grew excited. Really? I nodded, and she hugged and kissed me. Then she wanted to know why the tests couldn't be made now. I told her there wasn't time. I was due to be shipped overseas any day. Cursed war, she said. How long have you been a soldier, she asked. I said three years. She looked at me strangely. "Why are you still a private? You should be a captain or something." I said I wasn't ambitious. The rank might give you better pay, but you often lose your freedom. She said after thinking about it that I was right, that she'd never be a kept woman or marry just for money. "I like my independence too well." I said she spoke like a true Gemini, and she laughed.

Like Norma Jean, I was hooked on the movies. I had studied the Hollywood scene, worked in a photographic studio on Sunset Strip, and of course now was a celluloid commando at Fort Roach. So I knew a lot of movie stars personally—Gable, Alan Ladd, George Montgomery, Van Heflin, Joseph Cotten, Kent Smith, Ronald Reagan. But for present purposes, Leon Shamroy was the best industry contact I had. I'd worked with him on several training films, and I knew he'd do what he could when he saw Norma Jean's pictures.

Every detail of Hollywood fascinated Norma Jean, and she kept asking me what each actor I knew was *really like*. I suppose I had no particular insights into the stars I knew, but I did know them, and that's what mattered. Ladd, I told her, was a kind man, bothered by his shortness. Van Heflin, intense, rugged, and short-tempered; very much his own man. Joseph Cotten, I reported, I'd found hard to figure: very quiet, he kept much to himself and looked worried most of the time. He wasn't the friendliest person, but he was always polite and spoke in a soft voice.

"My, you're lucky," Norma Jean said.

"How's that?" I asked.

"Being with all those famous actors. Most people would give their eyeteeth to be in your shoes."

"It's not all that great." I shrugged. "They're just ordinary people like anyone else. They just happen to have famous names."

She gave my leg a hard rap. "Hey, don't be so calm about it," she said, and smiled at me.

I smiled back. "Don't molest the driver."

We were silent for a moment, then she looked at me quizzically, her face aglow from the distant sunset. "You're so easygoing, Shutterbug. I don't understand it. Doesn't anything bother you?"

I pulled up at the approaching roadside tavern. "Yes, my thirst. How about a cold beer?"

One other thing did bother me, though.

*July 15.* N.J. kept me waiting again this morning. As I am always prompt her slowness in getting started irritates me. I must have smoked three cigarettes waiting for her in the car. But as soon as she arrived, flashing those blue innocent eyes, and said in her whispering voice, hey, I'm sorry, I didn't mean to be late, well, you just can't stay angry with her. She has a habit also of saying surprising things unexpectedly, like last night in bed, in the middle of a clinch, she chirped, what's your wife like? I could have died. I gave her a description, and she asked if I loved her. I told her I wasn't sure, but I thought so. The trouble was Jeanne and I had no common interests. If we had something we could do together, besides sex, it might work out. You know, like pioneering a patch of wilderness somewhere. She said, like your island. I nodded. Yes, that might be just the thing to do the trick.

The insecurities of childhood had left a deeper mark on Norma Jean than showed outwardly. More than once I was awakened when she cried out in her sleep, troubled by her personal demons. I would gently cradle her in my arms and stroke her hair that smelled as sweet as wild honey and murmur, "It's all right, Sweetheart. Don't be afraid. Everything's all right." And in the morning, she would seem half ashamed, looking a little pale and apologizing in her shy and soft-spoken way.

I remember most clearly the very last night of our trip. We had hardly gone to sleep when I was awakened by a scream so shrill and penetrating that I jerked upright in bed. Norma Jean was sitting beside me, shivering and bathed in perspiration.

"It's that nightmare," she stammered. "Those men in white gowns . . ."

"Go on," I said softly. "What happened?" I thought letting her talk it out might help.

"They force me into a straitjacket and carry me out of the house. I'm screaming, 'I'm not crazy, I'm not crazy,' but they ignore me. I keep telling them there's nothing wrong with me, that I'm all right, that there must be some mistake. Their faces are blank, like somber masks, as they load me in a car that looks like a hearse only white. When we come to a brick building that looks like my old orphanage, we go through one black iron door after another and each door slams shut behind me. 'I don't belong here,' I shout. 'What are you doing to me?' They put me in a bleak room with barred windows and they go out and lock the iron door, leaving me in the straitjacket. 'I don't belong here,' I scream again and again, until I have no more breath."

She burst into a sob and buried her face in my chest. "Oh, Shutterbug," she cried, "it's so frightening. It's such a feeling of hopelessness."

I held her tight and stroked her hair as she cried. I didn't know what to say or how to comfort her. I just remember saying over and over, "It's all right, Sweetheart, it's all right."

Finally she lifted her tear-blurred eyes and stared at me. "It's a premonition. I just know it."

"No, no," I assured her. "Everybody has unpleasant dreams. Often the same ones. None of them amounts to a row of beans. Listen," I held her shoulders and looked at her, "you are perfectly normal. You've got talent and beauty. And you're going places. Besides, only sane people worry about going insane."

She gave a deep sigh and something seemed to relax inside her. "I hope so." She looked away, and I heard her catch her breath. "I do hope so," she whispered.

When she returned from the bathroom, looking more cheerful and with no trace of tears around her pretty eyes, she gave me her hand in a childlike way and smiled. "Thanks for the ear. I really didn't mean to unload on you. It just all boiled out."

"That's okay." I squeezed her hand and looked at her fondly. "I'm available any time. I think we always need someone who'll listen."

She got into bed and snuggled against me. "You know something, Shutterbug?"

"What?"

"I think you're a good influence."

"Why?"

"I'm really happy now. I don't feel alone anymore."

At that moment I felt we had found a new intimacy, one that in the years ahead would draw us together whenever we needed each other. We were both loners, and we understood each other.

Later that night. "Hey." The soft voice came through my sleep. "Are you awake?"

"I am now." I faced her, a bit disgruntled. "What's wrong?"

She rose up on her elbow. "I can't get to sleep. Have you any sleeping pills?"

"I'm afraid not."

She turned on the light and looked at me forlornly. "How about a game of poker?"

"Poker!" I exclaimed. "At this hour?" I glanced at my watch. It was ten past three.

Her voice came in a whisper. "There is something better." She nuzzled my cheek with her warm mouth.

"Yes, sleep." I pulled the covers around my shoulders. "Goodnight."

But now I felt restless, and tossed and turned fitfully. I just wasn't able to doze off. Neither could Norma Jean. "Okay," I said finally, "let's play poker."

Naked, we sat on the bed and she dealt the cards. After twenty minutes in which I didn't win a single hand, I was thoroughly depressed. "Did you work in Las Vegas or something? Where did you learn to play poker like that?"

She giggled. "From Jim. Merchant seamen are experts."

I was dreadfully tired and could hardly keep my eyes open. "Sorry. I've had enough," I said, and threw down the cards.

She looked at me with dreamy eyes. "But I'm not sleepy."

"Well, I am," I croaked.

"There must be something else we can do."

Her not very veiled suggestion came as no surprise, as her sexual appetite far exceeded my capacity to give her pleasure. "I'm much too tired. Really," I pleaded, and slipped between the sheets.

She leaned over me, displaying her magnificent breasts. "Maybe a massage would help. It usually does."

I looked up into her face. "Listen." I tried to remain calm. "We've got a long drive home tomorrow. I've got to be back at the base by three o'clock. It's terribly important. Otherwise I'll be AWOL."

She said softly, "I can drive, you know."

"I know you can, Sweetheart. But there's no point in both of us staying up all night." I fluffed up the pillow and pulled the covers over me. "For heaven's sake, please try to go to sleep!"

38

*July 1945.*

*July 1945.*

*July 17.* I had no expectation of trouble today as we headed homeward, enjoying the country outside Riverside. I just felt apprehensive about getting back to the base on time.

We were clipping along nicely when Norma Jean noticed a black and white terrier limping along the embankment and dragging a hind foot.

"Stop," she cried, grasping my arm.

I pulled off the highway. She jumped out and swept up the mutt in her arms, soothing its whimpers with love and affection.

"We'd better find a vet," she said. "I'm afraid its leg is broken." It looked as if the dog had been hit by a car.

I glanced nervously at my watch. We had only an hour and a half to get to Los Angeles. "We can't," I protested. "There isn't time. I'll be AWOL."

"Please," she begged, her eyes brimming with tears. "We can't leave him here. I can't stand to see an animal suffer." She hugged the little creature to her.

"Be reasonable," I pleaded. "Let the little guy go. I've barely enough time to get back to the base now."

She stared at me. "Reasonable!" she shouted. "You're the one not being reasonable! You're thinking only of yourself. This dog will get killed here on the highway. It's lucky he's alive now. Come on, let's find a vet."

My mind was whirling. I could see myself in the guardhouse over a dog. The whole thing was ridiculous.

I shook my head stubbornly. "No," I said, avoiding her eyes. "We'd better head for L.A." I got in the car and started the motor. "Are you coming?"

Her face was livid. "No." She was glaring at me. I'd never seen her so emphatic, nor her eyes so intent. "I'm going to find a vet." She began walking along the side of the highway, carrying the little dog in her arms.

That was more than I could stand. I pulled up beside her and opened the car door. "Oh, all right," I mumbled. "Get in."

She hopped in, cradling the dog in her lap. As we drove along silently, Norma Jean turned to me. She was smiling. "I knew this would happen. You're like me—just an old softie."

When we reached Riverside we stopped at a phone booth and got the address of a vet. But we didn't know the town, and it took us quite a while to find the Grove Dog and Cat Hospital. Then for almost an hour we sat impatiently in the waiting room while the dog's leg was set.

I told the doctor I had only ten dollars. "Will that do?"

He looked at my uniform, then at me. "Is it your dog?"

"No, it's a stray," I said.

The vet smiled. "We'll charge it off to charity."

But our problem still wasn't completely solved. When we got into the car with the dog, I stared at Norma Jean. "What are we going to do with it?" There was no collar or license tag to indicate the owner.

"I don't know." She gazed at the poor little thing asleep on her lap. "Aunt Ana can't keep it."

"I can't either," I replied. I checked the time again nervously. My heart sank. I was AWOL, and it was a queer, sick feeling.

The vet apparently had watched us in our quandary from the window. Now he came out to the car. "Why don't you leave him with me," he suggested. "I'll find him a home."

We both heaved a sigh of relief.

It was five-thirty when I pulled up at the entrance of Fort Roach. Alan Ladd, the sentry on duty, poked his head in the window. "Klein is looking for you, buddy. You'd better hurry." And he waved me though the gate.

I parked the car in front of Stage 4 and dashed up the wooden stairs to Klein's office. "Lord Jesus, Conover," Sergeant Klein began, "where in hell have you been? You were to report in at three."

I was squirming inside as he glared at me. "Sorry, sarge, my car broke down," I lied feebly.

"You should have allowed for the possibility. But since your overseas orders have arrived, I'll overlook your lateness." He picked up a paper on his desk and handed it to me. "These are your orders. You're to joint the 13th AAF Combat Camera unit in the Philippines."

"When? I asked, too afraid to look for myself.

"Immediately. Your train for San Francisco's Port of Embarkation departs from Union Station at nineteen-thirty hours. That's less than two hours from now. Be on it."

My heart jumped into my throat. I had wanted Norma Jean to have a beautiful portfolio of shots, and now it was out of the question: there were dozens of negatives to enlarge and print. After I visited the paymaster, an idea came to me. I called a friend of mine, Potter Hueth, a fellow photographer who had his own studio, and explained my predicament. He was willing to help. "God bless you, Huey," I said. Then I called Norma Jean and broke the news.

"Will your wife be at the station?" she asked hesitantly.

"No. She's in Palm Springs for her father's birthday."

"Okay. I'll be there," she breathed in her little girl voice.

"Great." And I hung up.

I looked at my watch. There wasn't enough time to drop off the negatives at Hueth's, so I bundled them up and dropped them in the mail at the Culver City Post Office. For some reason known only to God and the Post Office, they were never delivered. My pictures here present are those taken before the trip, and from the roll of film that remained in my Exakta.

I lived off base, in a pink stucco bungalow on West Vernon. I packed hurriedly, at the last moment squeezing in my duffel bag books by Thoreau, Goethe, and Keats. At least I would be in good company crossing the Pacific. I put the car keys on the kitchen table with a note to Jeanne, and then I called a cab.

At seven o'clock I was sitting on my duffel bag, scanning the people coming through the swinging doors of Union Station. Minutes skimmed by. After I butted out two cigarettes, there was still no sign of Norma Jean. My watch showed seven-thirty. I felt a sickening sense of disappointment. Where was she? Had she decided at the last minute not to come, or was she just late as usual? I paced nervously in front of Gate 11, searching the milling crowd for her face. The gatekeeper looked amused, but friendly. He asked, "You stood up, buddy?"

I nodded glumly, then showed him my orders. "If a young lady comes, will you . . .?"

He smiled sympathetically. "I will, soldier."

I passed through the gate to the side of the train as the short, stocky conductor at the end of the platform waved his hand and shouted, "All aboard." I look back once more and was disappointed. Then, just as I was climbing aboard the Pullman, Norma Jean came rushing towards me.

"Sorry," she said breathlessly, her eyes sparkling. "I got hung up in traffic."

We kissed hastily.

"Here, take this," I said, handing her a wad of bills. "Enroll in Miss Snively's modeling class. The Blue Book Agency I told you about. Until you get work. Okay?"

"No, I can't." Her soft blue eyes looked up at me. "You've done enough."

The train whistled.

I pressed the hundred dollars into her hand and jumped on the train.

"Call Potter Hueth," I said, looking down at her. "He's looking for a good model. And he'll talk to Miss Snively."

The train began to move. "You won't forget me, will you?"

"No." I smiled. "I'll never forget you."

There were half a million soldiers stockpiled in the Philippines ready for the invasion of Japan when the troopship I was on, the U.S.S. *Victory,* arrived in Manila. Two weeks later, the 13th AAF Combat Camera unit was disbanded, and I woke up one morning assigned to a motor pool.

I wrote to Norma Jean many times, but I received no reply. Either she had not received the letters or chose not to answer them for some personal reason. Perhaps a man had entered her life and these letters were embarrassing. I just didn't know, but I thought about it a lot as I drove officers around in a jeep and slowly developed an ulcerated tailbone from the jungle roads.

In time my lot improved: I was made chief librarian of the 13th Air Force, an ideal job for a bookworm. I had realized that on Luzon there were hundreds of thousands of soldiers in army camps and bivouacked in the jungles. They were growing restless, insolent, and insubordinate. There was little for them to do but get drunk and cause trouble. Books seemed a practical solution, and I proposed a scheme for a library (which happily involved purchasing trips to Australia). The plan was accepted, and soon I had a bibliographic empire, with branches on Leyte and Zamboanga. Not a bad way to spend the war.

I was discharged from the army in June 1946, just a year after I'd met Norma Jean. When I came home, Jeanne suggested, "Before you hang out your photographer's shingle, let's take a trip. It'll give us a chance to get to know each other again."

"Fine," I said.

"Where shall we go?"

I didn't hesitate for a moment. "British Columbia. I'd like you to see a dream of mine."

46

*"Playing those sexy screen roles, they think you want to keep at it off screen, too. Well, I'm not made that way. Sex isn't that important to me."*

Wallace Island. Uninhabited, nearly two hundred acres, a haven of giant firs, grassy meadows, and secluded coves. Our only spoken plan was to spend the day picnicking. But long before it was time to come back that afternoon, we started making plans—quite serious plans—about where we'd build our house, where we'd plant our garden, where we'd put up cottages to rent to summer visitors.

Fortunately, the island was for sale.

The price—$17,500—was steep, much too steep for us. But our minds were made up. We raced back to Los Angeles, sold our pink stucco bungalow to cover the down payment, and waved goodbye to our families. We bought an old lifeboat in Victoria, moved our goods onto the island, and set up camp.

Few people knew less about boats or the sea, carpentry or plumbing, or the rudiments of country life than we did. Such tools as hammer, shovel, and axe we had seen only in hardware stores. But after several years of much hard labor and considerable bungling, we built a house, wharf, store, and six attractive guest cottages. My journals of those years recorded our adventures and later became the basis of my first book, *Once Upon an Island*. The

49

Gentlemen Prefer Blondes, *1953*.

resort kept us so busy both winter and summer that we lost all interest in the outside world, leaving the island only for the occasional visit to Victoria for supplies.

On one such trip, in December of 1952, Jeanne saw my name in a movie magazine. The article was the life story of Marilyn Monroe, a film star we had only heard about on the radio. Jeanne scanned the piece and asked curiously, "Do you know anyone by the name of Norma Jean Dougherty?"

"Yes," I admitted. "Why?"

"She's Marilyn Monroe."

"Really?" I couldn't believe it. "Are you sure?"

She held up the magazine. "Look for yourself." And she pointed to the words.

There in print the star gave credit to David Conover and his beautiful photographs for launching her career. I was dumbstruck. My Norma Jean a movie star! It was incredible—yet I had known when I first photographed her that she was something special, more than just a clean-cut girl with a good figure and a pretty face. Maybe because I had fallen for her. I don't know. I only know I had never encountered anyone who wanted success so badly.

"Where did you meet her?" Jeanne asked.

"In a defense plant," I said, "during World War II. I took some shots of her. She said she wanted to be an actress."

Jeanne laughed. "Well, she sure succeeded. Marilyn's one of the biggest stars in Hollywood."

We went to California that winter to see our parents and my brother, Austin, a reporter for the *Hollywood Citizen-News*.

*January 13.* When we reached L.A. this afternoon I could understand why I left here and gave up a car for a boat. I prefer the sea all around me instead of people. Catherine [Austin's wife] looks good, but Austin looks terrible. His eyes and face are strained from overwork. The newspaper racket has aged him drastically. After dinner I asked him if he could get me into 20th Century Fox. Sure, he said. No trouble at all. I'll get you a press pass. Any particular reason? I kidded him. I'd like to see an old girlfriend who works there. Who? he asked. I think she's called Marilyn, I said.

The next day as I drove along Olympic Boulevard to the studio I kept asking myself, Will she remember me? Will she remember me after seven years?

The set of *Gentlemen Prefer Blondes* was crowded but silent. Marilyn and Jane Russell were doing a scene together, and you could almost hear a pin drop. Standing there, watching, I could barely see her behind so many heads. Suddenly I heard a scream: "SHUTTERBUG! OH, SHUTTERBUG!" Charging through the wall of people, Marilyn threw her arms around me and showered my face with kisses.

So she hadn't forgotten me, and her gratitude was clearly expressed. But the director, Howard Hawks, was ready to explode. "Now what!" he exclaimed, throwing his arms into the air.

I looked at Marilyn. "I didn't mean—" the words stuck in my throat—"to interrupt," I finally finished.

"Silly, you haven't," she reassured me. "There isn't anyone I want to see more than you." The technicians were glaring at me now and Hawks was chomping on his cigar.

I looked nervously around me. "I don't think anyone else will agree."

"Yes, they will. When I tell them." She took my arm and led me through the crowd onto the set.

"Listen, fellas," she announced. "This is the photographer who discovered me working on an assembly line. I want you to meet David Conover."

The tense atmosphere immediately relaxed and became jovial. Everyone came over smiling to shake my hand. Flashbulbs went off. Hands clapped my back. I was bombarded with questions. It was as if for a moment I were the celebrity.

"It's good publicity," Marilyn whispered and gave that funny little laugh of hers. "Just relax."

How could I? I was as tense as a railroad tie. Everybody was staring at us or, rather, at me and my baggy tweed suit. "You sure can pick 'em!" Howard Hawks was wringing my hand. "You'd better come to work for us. Zanuck could use a good talent scout."

Jane Russell smiled. "You'll have to go some to find anyone as beautiful as Marilyn."

"And as talented," Natasha Lytess, Marilyn's drama coach, added soberly.

Then it all became quiet while Jane and I stood behind the big lights and watched Norma Jean rehearse the number "Diamonds Are a Girl's

*With Jane Russell in* Gentlemen Prefer Blondes, *1953.*

Best Friend." N.J. looked stunning in a long sequined dress, very skin tight, revealing every curve of her gorgeous body. "It's funny," Jane said to me, "Diamonds are the last thing on her mind. That gal would rather have several good books." Later I asked N.J. to come out to the car so I could get a picture of her. When she saw "Wallace Island Resort" on the station wagon, she said, "Hey, you did corral your island. Are you happy?" I said, "Yes—very." I snapped her picture by the car, and a studio photographer took some of both of us. "Hey, I'd better go. Drop by the hotel tonight and we'll catch up on one another." I can't get used to calling her Marilyn. Grady Johnson, a Fox P.R. man, walked up. "Man," he said to me, "I've never seen anyone so happy to see somebody. It'll make all the papers. If all the stars were like her I'd be out of a job." I was curious. "Why?" I asked. "She has an uncanny knack of getting publicity."

After she disappeared into the sound stage, it occurred to me I had forgotten to ask her where she was staying. Grady Johnson told me, then asked, "What do you think of Marilyn? She must have changed a lot since the last time you saw her."

"Yes," I said thoughtfully. "She's grown even more beautiful."

Driving along Sunset Boulevard that evening towards the Beverly Hills Hotel, where Marilyn was staying, I was bothered by Johnson's words. Was Marilyn really glad to see me, or had her performance been mainly for publicity?

I asked for her room number at the hotel desk.

"Sorry," the clerk said, "Miss Monroe doesn't see visitors."

I asked the clerk to give Miss Monroe my name. She did, then put down the phone and told me again, "No visitors."

This was awfully strange after the warm welcome at the studio. Maybe, after all, that show of affection had been just a publicity stunt. No, I thought, Norma Jean was too honest for that. But why had she decided not to see me? Surely she hadn't changed that much. I sat down in the lounge and wondered what to do.

A bellboy walked by with a huge basket of flowers. Could they be for her? From a distance, I followed him down the corridors until he stopped and knocked at a door, then disappeared inside. I crept closer and heard a woman's voice say, "Thank you very much." The voice was Marilyn's—no doubt about it.

*With the author on the set of* Gentlemen Prefer Blondes,
*January 14, 1953.*

I waited, wondering if I should invade her privacy. Had she wanted to see me, she would have asked me to come to her room. But I knew I could never go home without seeing her again. So I knocked on the door.

"Who is it?" she asked.

"David . . . David Conover."

The door cracked open and Marilyn looked at me sullenly. "What do you want?"

I felt awkward and embarrassed. "Nothing . . . not a thing.." I tried not to stutter. "I'd just like that chat you promised me."

The door opened a little farther. Marilyn was barefoot and without makeup. She was wearing a white bathrobe, and her tousled golden hair fell onto her forehead. She looked me in the eye and after a painful pause said quietly, "Well, I really don't believe you, but come in for a few minutes." She motioned to the green velvet sofa near the fireplace, opposite a matching chair. Heavy blue draperies were carefully drawn across the windows.

I sat down uneasily. I didn't understand her hostile manner. This wasn't at all like the Norma Jean I had known. Marilyn walked over and stared down at me, and now I could see a trace of sadness beneath the anger in her eyes. "I thought you were something special. But you're no different from all the rest."

"What do you mean?"

"You want something. Everybody wants something," she said vehemently. "You're the last person who I thought would try to use me."

"That's not true," I snapped, "and you know it."

"Isn't it?" Her smile was bitter, her face taut. "I saw the way you lapped up the publicity on the set. How you insisted on having your picture taken with me beside your resort wagon. Isn't that why you're here? To pick up some free publicity?" Her voice was brittle. I had never heard her speak so harshly.

"Heavens, no!" I cried. "It was you who said it would be good publicity. The only reason I came was to see my friend Norma Jean again."

She sat on the sofa in a sort of daze and stared at her hands. "I don't know what's true anymore. All I know is I'm always being used. I've gotten to the point where I distrust everyone. It's terrible when you can't tell who your friends are. Honestly, there's not a soul I can confide in. Even Natasha, who's been like a mother to me, I can't trust anymore. Now you, of all people."

"But you can trust me," I said gently. "I'd never use you. Remember that day in Barstow when I said, 'I don't want any favors'? Well, that's the way it is and always will be. Do you understand?"

Slowly she nodded and looked up at me. Her eyes were brimming with tears. "Oh, Shutterbug," she sobbed, "forgive me. I'm such a fool. I was wrong . . . so very wrong." I held her close and stroked her hair as I had done years before.

At last she sat up and tried to smile. "I'm sorry, Shutterbug. I shouldn't have jumped on you."

"That's okay," I said, squeezing her hand. "I'm glad I found you."

"So am I. It's nice to talk to somebody without watching every word you say. Why, I can't even be myself in front of my own maid. Isn't that stupid?"

I agreed. Then Marilyn got up. "I think we should celebrate our reunion. I'll get some champagne."

She set two glasses on the coffee table and I popped open the Dom Perignon. The cork struck the ceiling and came down on my head. As I rubbed the sore spot, Marilyn began to laugh. "This will deaden the pain," she said as she filled the glasses.

She seemed now more like the girl I remembered. I held up my glass. "To your fabulous success, Sweetheart." She smiled brightly as we sipped our drinks. Then she put down her glass, frowning slightly. "You know, I'm still mad at you. Why didn't you write?"

"I did, many times. But I never received an answer."

She shrugged. "Oh, well. We're together again. That's all that matters." She smiled at me fondly.

I was eager to know how she'd made it to the top. "Now, tell me everything that's happened since that day at Union Station."

"Oh, my. So much . . . let's see. Well, to begin, Potter Hueth was a godsend. He got me into Miss Snively's modeling agency. Then, after a lot of modeling jobs, I made several magazine covers, thanks to André de Dienes's photographs. Tom Kelley helped me too, when I posed for that nude calendar. I didn't want to do it. But he was such a dear, and I was broke. The fifty bucks paid my room rent for three months."

Marilyn leaned back on the sofa. She took a sip of champagne and went on. "My first real break came when the agent, Harry Lipton, took me on. He suggested that I see Ben Lyon at Fox, who gave me a screen test. It turned out so well I got a contract—seventy-five dollars a week." She laughed. "Say, I bet you can't guess who filmed my screen test."

"No, tell me," I said—but I thought I knew.

"Your friend, Leon Shamroy. He was so kind and gentle. A very sweet man. And you know something else? I just finished making *Niagara* with another friend of yours, Joseph Cotten. It's funny. Though you weren't in my life all these years, you played a very important part in it. We seem destined to be always good friends even if we are miles apart."

"To our friendship," I toasted, my glass in the air.

She touched her glass to mine and smiled. "May it last forever." And we drank heartily.

"Hey! Remember Adele Jergens? The girl you were photographing the same time as me? Well, she starred in one of my first pictures, *Ladies of the Chorus,* and she's doing great. Isn't that neat? You've got two stars to your credit."

"How many pictures have you made?" I asked.

She thought for a moment. "Nineteen so far. But acting doesn't get any easier. Every time I step before the camera, I get so choked up, so scared I can hardly get the lines out. I try so hard to please everybody and it's a terrible worry. Now, if just once, I could hear a chorus of people say, 'Hi there, Marilyn. You're doing fine, keep going,' well, then, I might get a feeling of security about this acting business. At any rate, it would help."

"Doesn't experience build confidence?" I asked.

"I guess I'm different." She shrugged and swallowed her drink. "When I start a new picture, it's like learning to act all over again. Maybe it's because I know that my screen image doesn't at all represent me, my *real* me, the way I feel, the way I act and talk. It's something very much apart from my personality, this being a dumb sexy blonde. I'm neither dumb, nor any sexier that any other woman. But they don't think I can act, so I'm stuck playing the sextress. That's my own word. I coined it myself. I'm not an actress. I'm a *sextress!* And it's really awful."

"But you've got success, fame, money . . ."

"It's an awful life, I mean, in the way people treat you and think about you. Like, just because you're playing those sexy screen roles, they think you want to keep at it off screen, too. Well, I'm not made that way. Sex isn't that important to me. I used to trust everybody and got asked out a lot, but I found out it was only for one reason. So I rarely go out anymore. I hate being treated that way. I want to be liked and loved for myself. And for myself alone."

I wanted to know who helped her the most to become a star.

"Johnny Hyde," she said immediately. "He was the top agent in Hollywood. He got me good parts and looked after me with style. He was one classy guy. But he wanted more than friendship and insisted that we get married. I couldn't. I just wasn't in love with him. I believed only love meant marriage. Even when he offered me his fortune, I still refused. It was the hardest thing I've ever done in my life. Then he died of a heart attack. I felt partly to blame, and I cried for days after the funeral. He was like a father, so kind . . . understanding . . .''

Tears were streaming down her cheeks. She pulled a Kleenex from her pocket and began dabbing her face. "I cry too easily, don't I? I'm sorry."

"You needn't be." I kissed the tip of her nose. "It shows you've got a big heart."

"That's been my main problem. It seems I'm always helping people out. Or falling in love and out of love. Sometimes all three at the same time."

I was curious. "Were you ever in love with somebody who didn't love you?"

"Yes," she replied without hesitation. "My vocal teacher at Columbia, Fred Karger. He was very shy and reserved and almost as unsure of himself as I was. Shortly after our first dinner date I discovered I was in love with him. I wanted to marry him. Even his mother and sister encouraged the match. I did everything to persuade him. But the more I begged him to, the more he withdrew from me. Still, we remained friends. He taught me how to sing, and for that I'll always be grateful."

She rose to her feet. "Now to show you how glad I am you're here," she said smiling, "I'll get into something special just for you."

Then, to my astonishment, Marilyn slipped the bathrobe off her shoulders and let it fall to the floor. She stood there naked and unembarrassed, smiling innocently. "Do you think my figure has improved?" she asked softly.

Then she walked towards the bedroom, the round curves of her buttocks brushing against each other like the wings of a butterfly. "I won't be long, Shutterbug," she said as she disappeared behind the door, leaving behind the aroma of her perfume that made the room smell like a florist's shop full of exotic blooms. I liked the way she said "Shutterbug." It was as if she whispered it through a soft piece of silk.

I knew now I'd have to find a way to catch up on her past films. At the studio today her dress and makeup had made her look like a gorgeous hussy. But now, except for the platinum hair, Marilyn looked much the same as the Norma Jean I remembered. The years of struggle and hard work had left no apparent marks. Even her voice sounded the same: sweet, soft, childlike, with a touch of shyness and slight hesitation that seemed to me—a firm romantic—the essence of femininity.

When Marilyn came back to the room, she looked divine. She was wearing a low-cut satin dress that seemed painted on her astonishing figure. She stood in front of me and smiled, like a child looking for praise.

"How do I look?" she asked, her eyes sparkling.

"Stunning," I said. I had no other words.

The door chime rang and another huge basket of flowers arrived, long-stemmed velvety roses. Marilyn put them on a table and quickly read the accompanying card. The message did not seem to please her.

"Oh, no," she groaned, "not again."

"What's wrong?"

She was frowning. "It's always the same message—'I love you, I love you.' It comes every day. Day in and day out. As if I didn't know it."

"Who's the lucky man?"

"Don't you know?" She filled her glass again. Her capacity was amazing; it seemed to have little effect upon her except to make her more talkative. I had to decline a refill, because I was getting lightheaded and I wanted to remember this evening as fully as possible.

"How would I?" I said. "I'm not up on Hollywood life."

She giggled. "I think the whole world knows but you. Well, it's Joe DiMaggio."

"Has he proposed?"

"Dozens of times." She sipped her drink. "He practically camps on my doorstep."

I looked at her. "Do you love him?"

"I don't know. He's very sweet and kind. And very much a gentleman. But sometimes he's so boring I could scream. All he knows and talks about is baseball. That's why I'm not sure. I don't want to go through life fielding his baseballs."

She nestled the card among the flowers, then sat down beside me. "Now let's talk about you. What's your island like?"

I talked to her about the big firs, the twisted driftwood and sandy beaches, the ever changing shoreline dotted with hidden coves, miles of wooded trails where deer and mink and eagles were constantly seen. How we now had six lovely cottages, each secluded for privacy, each with its own view of the woods and the sea.

"It sounds like paradise," she exclaimed. "How lucky you and Jeanne are. Is she here with you?"

"She's staying with her parents in Pomona. I'm staying here in town with my brother."

She looked at me curiously. "Does he write a column for the *Citizen-News?*"

"Yes."

"Funny. I've met him several times. I had no idea Austin was your brother. He's a good reporter."

I grinned at her. "Better mind yourself. I'm going to have him keep an eye on you."

She laughed. Then she said excitedly, "Hey, why don't you become my business manager? Help me manage my career, the money and everything. I never know what to do with it. You're about the only person I can completely trust."

"Thanks. The offer is appreciated. But—"

"You're too much in love with your island, right?"

"It's the kind of life I've always wanted. I don't think anything could make me give it up. Not even any amount of money."

"I don't understand," she said. "What makes living all alone on an island so terrific?"

I thought for a moment. "Freedom, I suppose. When I get up in the morning I'm free to choose any job I want to do. Or I can just loaf, swim, fish, write. It's very exhilarating to know you have complete control over your life."

"Do you still keep a journal?"

I nodded. "In fact, I've nearly finished a book."

"Hey, that's great. What's it about?"

"Guess!" I smiled. "It's called *Once Upon an Island.*"

"I should have known." She laughed. "Now you'll have to write about me."

"I'd like to someday," I said. "After I become a professional writer."

"That's what you really want to be, isn't it?"

I nodded, and stood up. "I'd better push off. I know you have a busy schedule tomorrow."

She rose, and her eyes met mine. "Come and see me whenever you can. Won't you?" she said with a forlorn look, as if she didn't want me to go. I suddenly felt a great tenderness for her. She sounded so lonely, so desperate for companionship.

"I will," I said, and smiled at her.

She touched my cheek with her hand. "When you call or want to see me,

spell your name backwards. It'll be easier for me."

"Why?"

"Joe gets very jealous."

She slipped her arm through mine and walked me to the door. For a moment we studied each other closely, neither of us knowing what to say. I wanted to tell her that I had always been in love with her, but I didn't. That would only complicate both our lives, as dissimilar as night and day. Instead, I embraced her warmly, without kissing her. "Take care, Sweetheart."

"And you, too, Shutterbug. It was wonderful to see you." She held me tightly for a moment, then quickly kissed my cheek and whispered, "Hey, now. Let's keep in touch."

On January 16 I wrote in my journal:

It was quite a thrill to see my name yesterday in the *Herald-Express:* "Man who discovered Marilyn Monroe gets a kiss from star." I was so proud. I showed the paper to Mother. Son, she said, haven't you got anything better to do than associate with the likes of her? That took the wind out of my sails.

*Leaving Lenox Hill Hospital, New York, after gynecological surgery, June 26, 1959.*

*"I live like a goldfish in a bowl.
There's little in my life that's
private. So it'll be kinda fun
keeping our 'us' between ourselves."*

April is a spoiled child—an elusive blessing or a curse. One day it's raw and windy, the next warm and shining. Each morning we are faced with a weighty decision. Do we take off our long johns or leave them on?

The first geese journeyed over the island yesterday. They brought the clear sparkling air. There's a nip in the shade, where winter still reigns, but the yard is sun-filled and the grass ankle deep, diamonded with dew. No four walls could hold me inside. Jeanne was starting the mower. "Let's go fishing," I pleaded. "To hell with the grass."

Still, there were always tasks to be done.

*April 19.* Thank God work on the wharf is finished. I thought I'd never get the logs under the floats. I am so clumsy I lost my hammer again today and it took me an hour with a grappling hook to recover it off the bottom.

Perhaps as a reward for finishing the wharf, the next day I heard from Marilyn. I wrote the essence of her letters into my journal, often from memory; I had a habit of losing things, a habit Marilyn shared with me. Jane Russell once said, "Marilyn is always losing something—address book, driver's license, grocery lists. Sometimes she even forgets where she parked her car."

Marilyn was a phoner rather than a writer. She didn't like to write because her poor handwriting and spelling made her feel bad that she hadn't finished high school. Her sensitivity about "not being educated" kindled in her a keen determination to read and learn.

As before, I had begun introducing great books to her, this time by mail. With each one I would include a brief explanation why the book deserved to be read and the reasons that prompted the author to write it. In this letter she reported that one such classic had caused her unexpected embarrassment (spring 1953, of course, was the peak of McCarthy's witch hunt):

Tolstoy's *War and Peace* was not easy reading, she wrote, but she was gobbling up the pages; she'd never read a book that made her think so much. At the studio, during a break in the shooting the director, Jean Negulesco, had asked her what she was reading, and she told him Tolstoy in glowing words. He said that she shouldn't be seen reading such stuff, that it might get her into trouble. That really confused Marilyn and she asked Negulesco why. He said that people would think she was a radical—a red. She wrote that he seemed upset that she didn't know what a communist was, and she asked me if they weren't a Russian ball club.

On the following page was a postscript that touched me deeply. Calling me "Shutterbug," she wrote that she hoped I didn't mind, but she thought our relationship should be kept secret—just between her and me and God, if he's listening. She went on to say it wasn't just Joe's jealousy that worried her, but all the schemers and plotters around her. So she thought it would be safer this way. She said she knew I would agree, because more than anyone else I wanted what was best for her. She felt she lived like a goldfish in a bowl, with little in her life that was private. So, she concluded, it would be, as she said, "kinda fun" keeping our "us" between ourselves.

Jane Russell had also said of Marilyn, "She lives in her own little world, often cut off from reality." These dreamlike states came and went; they were more frequent with people who disliked her, or those she felt uncomfortable with. She was sensitive to the attitudes of others, and only by self-imposed reverie could she cope with such people without being rude. Nunnally John-son, the producer-writer of *How to Marry a Millionaire*, was often the target of Marilyn's somnambulistic moods, and he once remarked, "You can't talk to her. Talking to her is like talking to somebody ten feet under water. Between you and her there is a thick wall of cotton. You can't get through to her."

Marilyn often retreated behind a mask of innocence—a role she played with equal dexterity on and off screen—when she was uncertain, needed sympathy, or wished to confuse her detractors. On one occasion, she had a brief but difficult scene to shoot, and time after time she fluffed her lines or forgot them. After the twenty-sixth take, her director tried a different ap-proach. He walked over to Marilyn and took her hand. "Relax, honey. We'll try it again tomorrow. Just don't worry."

Marilyn's big blue eyes looked up, puzzled. "Why? Is anything wrong?"

Worried? No. Not about reshooting. She was more concerned about Natasha Lytess, standing in the shadows behind the lights, whether she'd nod her head or shake it after each take. Natasha had brought her famous pupil from a relative nobody to a somebody with remarkable dedication and finesse, and she was as much a perfectionist as Marilyn. It was only natural that when Natasha shook her head, Marilyn would demand that the scene be reshot, even though the director was satisfied.

This infuriated both Negulesco and Johnson. Retakes were wearying and time-consuming, causing the picture to go far over budget. Johnson ordered Natasha off the set. Marilyn retaliated with her only weapon: she didn't report for work the next day.

Marilyn called me that evening and explained what had happened. She was nervous and frightened. "Do you think I did right?" Her small voice quavered.

"Of course," I said. "You've got to stand up to those bastards. It's the only way."

Without its star, the studio quickly capitulated and reinstated Natasha. What Johnson failed to understand, as had so many other studio officials, was that Marilyn was simply—and overwhelmingly—frightened by her lack of education and experience as an actress.

"What's happened to her," said Billy Wilder, the first director to recognize this, "is enough to drive almost anybody slightly daffy, even someone whose background has armored her with poise and calmness. But you take a girl like Marilyn, who's never really had a chance to learn, who's never really had a chance to live, and you suddenly confront her with a Frankenstein's monster of herself built of fame and publicity and notoriety, and naturally she's a little mixed up and made giddy by it all."

By this time I was again well informed about what was happening in the movie capital, as I'd been in my Fort Roach days. From my island I subscribed to the *Los Angeles Times*, the *Hollywood Reporter*, numerous film magazines; and, most important, Austin always kept me abreast of Marilyn's latest activities. At the *Hollywood Citizen-News*, his desk was next to that of Sidney Skolsky, the highly respected Hollywood columnist and a friend of Marilyn's who frequently escorted her to parties and premières. So I often heard rumors and choice bits of gossip long before they became common knowledge.

Thanks to Marilyn my Robinson Crusoe way of life had now taken on fresh excitement. It was as far removed from Hollywood as though I lived on another planet, and yet I had a pipeline to the life of a movie star. It was as if I lived two separate lives. To be both "a part of" and "apart from" appealed to my romantic nature. The days were no longer a blur of self-centeredness. While I painted a boat or fixed a water pump, my mind would travel to Stage 2 of the Fox lot or to Schwab's Drug Store, where Marilyn would pick up Skolsky and drive him around town.

In June, Marilyn phoned again. "Hi, handsome," came her low breathless voice over the radiophone. "I'm heading up your way in a few days. Think we can get together?" She sounded down in the dumps despite her cheery words, as if she needed someone to talk to.

"Sure," I said. "Where?"

"Banff. I'll be making a film there called *River of No Return*. Is that close to you?" She didn't know her geography, but that didn't matter. If she was going to be in Canada, Banff was close by.

"Yes."

"That's good. I'd like so much to see you."

"I'd like to see you, too."

She told me the date she'd be arriving and the name of her hotel. "I'll have a room reserved for you next to mine. Okay?" Her voice seemed more natural, more relaxed now.

"That'll be great," I replied. "I'll see you at Banff on Wednesday."

The huge Air Canada DC-6 skimmed me across the Rockies to the little town huddled among the mountains, where I hailed a taxi to drive me to the Banff Springs Hotel. It was getting towards dusk. The driver was excited— he could talk only about the movie being shot there. "If you're lucky, you might get to see Marilyn Monroe," he said. "She's some babe, believe me. Are you one of the film crew?"

"No."

"Just curious. I thought you might have something to do with it. I'd sure like to meet her. Have you got a room booked?"

"Yes."

"That's good," he said. "This place is crawling with film people. Robert Mitchum, Rory Calhoun—lots of celebrities. Not a room anywhere."

At the hotel desk, I asked, "Have you a reservation for Conover?"

The clerk checked. "Sorry, I'm afraid not." I couldn't figure it. Marilyn always kept her word. Maybe she had just forgotten.

I didn't have much hope without a reservation, but I thought I'd inquire anyway. "Do you have a room available?"

"No, I'm sorry. We're booked solid."

My next question was absolutely hopeless, but I asked it anyway. "Could I have Marilyn Monroe's room number, please?"

The clerk looked amazed. "Sorry, sir. We're not allowed to give out that information."

Crestfallen, I went into the bar, ordered a Scotch on the rocks, and tried to figure out what to do. Should I go to a phone on the off chance that I might be connected with Marilyn's room, or just sit in the lobby and wait for her to show up? After I finished my second drink, I decided to station myself on a divan in the lobby where she'd be sure to see me. I had no way of knowing if she was even in the hotel at the time, so I tried to watch both the elevators and the front entrance. A few moments later, I heard shrill cries and looked up to see Rory Calhoun being mobbed by a group of teenage autograph seekers. They pulled and tugged at his clothing like vultures for even the slightest souvenir. He was being as pleasant and accommodating as he could in the circumstances, and I felt sorry for him. It wasn't easy being a movie star, I thought, as Calhoun finally made a dash for the safety of a waiting elevator minus his tie, cuff links, and shoe laces.

It had been an exhausting day. I had traveled from the island by small boat, by car and ferry, then by plane. Soon sleep overwhelmed me. I awoke some time later and looked at my watch. It was 10:30 P.M. Then I saw the note on my lap.

Short and sweet, signed only with her initial, it explained the mystery. The room number, she'd scribbled, was 817—and the reservation was under *Revonoc*.

Stupid me, I'd forgotten!

I went up to my room, freshened up, and knocked gently on the door nearest to mine, hoping it was the right one.

"Who is it?" came a girl's gentle voice.

"Mr. Revonoc."

The door flew open. A barefoot Marilyn looked beautiful and cool, a red silk robe wrapped hastily around her. Even without cosmetics she glowed.

After we kissed, she said to me, "You looked so weary, I didn't want to wake you. Come on in." She took my hand and led me into her room, then poured each of us a tumblerful of Dom Perignon.

"Cheers." I held up my glass.

She responded a little weakly. As we sat on the sofa sipping our drinks, I could see something was bothering Marilyn. Her eyes looked tired and strained, as if she hadn't slept for days. "Okay, Sweetheart," I said, "spill it."

She did. "I'm so damned miserable and lonely. If you hadn't come I wouldn't have known what to do. Joe and I had a fight just before I left. I've never seen him so angry and upset. He took his clothes and walked out on me." She bit her lip to stop it from trembling, then suddenly she buried her face against my shoulder and broke into tears.

"I'm sorry." I just held her and stroked her head. "Was Joe putting pressure on you to marry him?" It had been obvious to me and to other people in a position to know, like Sidney Skolsky, that Marilyn felt ambivalent about Joe.

"Yes," she sobbed. "He's tired of waiting, tired of Hollywood, tired of all the publicity. He wants to settle down and raise a family in San Francisco. But I can't make up my mind."

I lifted her face. The tears were silvery streaks on her cheeks. "Do you love him?" I asked.

"Yes," she answered. "But that isn't the problem."

"What is, then?"

The tears had stopped and there was a blank look of despair in her eyes. "I can't see myself married to Joe. I really can't."

"Why not?"

She tried to smile. "I hate spaghetti."

I almost laughed.

"And baseball," she added.

"Your friend, Jane Russell, is married to a famous professional football player. Isn't she happy?"

"Oh, yes, very."

"So . . ."

"But all Joe does is watch TV."

"You could study your lines for next day's shooting."

"I guess I could."

"Well, Sweetheart, look at it this way. If you marry him, you'll have both a lover and a friend. If you don't, you'll end up with neither."

She thought about that for a moment, then decided to change the subject. "Does your wife know you're seeing me?"

"I suspect so."

"Oh, I'm sorry," Marilyn said. "I hope it won't upset things."

"No, not really. She has her own friends. I see no reason why I shouldn't have mine."

"How's the book coming?"

"Slowly." I sighed. "I just don't know how to plot or write dialogue. So I've signed up for a correspondence course in professional writing at the University of Oklahoma. It should help."

I knew that Marilyn had developed the habit of walking around a room nude. Now she slipped off her robe and stood in front of a full-length mirror. She cupped her breasts, studied them with an expression of uncertainty, and asked, "Are they too large?"

"Heavens, no," I reassured her. "They're perfect."

A small incident. But with every step Marilyn took in her life she needed constant reassurance. Insecurity was the root of her gravest problems. Throughout her career, she was unable to trust her own judgment of her work, always depending on a coach during every film. This infuriated her directors, who were in far better position to evaluate her performance and delineate her natural charm. After I had seen her movies, I told Marilyn not once but innumerable times that she underrated her magic in front of the camera. I don't know if she ever could believe me.

Our conversation turned to the movie she was making in Banff. Marilyn didn't like the script of *River of No Return* (she was unusually good at judging scripts and film roles), and she cared even less for Otto Preminger, whom she referred to as a pompous ass. After describing the story to me, she sighed, "At least it's a dramatic role for a change. Even if it is a soapy Western."

Marilyn told me about the scene she had shot that day on the Athabasca River, and that in between takes two boys had come by on bicycles. "Do

71

you know what I did? Well, I borrowed one of the bicycles and took off for an hour."

"Preminger must have been furious," I said. "Why did you do that?"

"He barred Natasha from the set," Marilyn said angrily. "The bastard thinks he's God almighty. So I'm screwing up the picture so badly he'll never get another job at Fox." Then she told me how, a few days earlier, she had deliberately wrecked a scene at a crucial moment during the filming by announcing that she had to go to the bathroom.

I was disturbed. This did not seem to be a reasonable way to handle the situation and, like much of Marilyn's behavior, it was petty and childish. "Listen, Sweetheart. Get in touch with Zanuck," I suggested. "Tell him how upset you are and that you can't finish the film without Natasha." This battle with Preminger was only one of many she fought with her directors and producers to defend Natasha and, later, Paula Strasberg.

She liked my idea. "Hey, I'll do that right now. Maybe I can catch him at home."

While I opened another bottle of Dom Perignon, Marilyn got Zanuck on the phone. A few minutes later she came over to me, her face beaming. "It's all fixed. He said Preminger owed him a bunch of favors. Natasha will be reinstated."

I handed her a glass of champagne. "Well, here's to Mr. Zanuck," I toasted.

"To Mr. Z," she said halfheartedly, raising her glass. "I didn't think it would be that easy."

"Why not?" I asked. "You had a legitimate complaint."

She laughed. "Complaints? I've got dozens of them. I'm underpaid, I don't get the right parts, and I'm not treated with the respect that I deserve. But the bastard won't listen to me. He avoids me like the plague."

She took a large swallow of champagne and went on. "None of this would have happened if Johnny Hyde was alive. None of it. Johnny was the best agent in Hollywood. He took care of me. He believed in me."

Marilyn had told me about Hyde before, and I knew what he meant to her. "He must have been a fine man," I said.

"Yes. And a fighter. He knew how to make those big shots squirm until he got what he wanted. When he died, all of a sudden, I felt abandoned. I thought my career was over. I just didn't know how to promote myself, you know, deal with the studio brass. I didn't want to go on playing dumb blondes. Johnny was against that, too. He thought I could become a serious actress." She stared into her empty glass and said, "God, it's awful when no one believes in you."

I put my hand on hers. "The public does. Millions of people believe in you and adore you."

"I know," she said softly. "It's the one thing that keeps me going. The public has never let me down."

"They never will," I assured her. "Do you know why?"

"No, not really."

"Because people see in Marilyn Monroe mostly Norma Jean. The girl on the same block who became famous without becoming a phony. You're not a Zanuck star or a Fox star. You're the people's star." I squeezed her hand and smiled. "Now is anything else bothering you?"

"Yes." Marilyn grinned. "I'm hungry. Aren't you?"

I agreed wholeheartedly, and she had supper sent up to her suite. By the time we had finished eating, it was well past midnight. We were both tired and sleepy. "You're lucky." Marilyn sat back and yawned. "You can sleep tomorrow. But I've got to get up five and go to work."

In the bedroom, I tucked the covers around her and kissed her goodnight. "I feel a lot happier now." She smiled up at me. "Having Natasha on the set means a great deal to me. I'm not a very good actress yet. But with her help I know I will be." As I turned to go, she asked me to come to the set the next day. "I want to see you as much as possible." I said, "I'll be there." Then I slipped off quietly and tumbled into bed.

It was almost noon before I woke the next morning. When I was about ready to leave for the set, I heard someone at Marilyn's door. Curious, I looked in the hall. There was Marilyn, on crutches. I helped her inside. "What happened?" I demanded.

She collapsed on the bed. "I hurt my foot. I think it's a bruised muscle. That's what the studio nurse said when she felt my ankle."

"How did you do it?"

"I fell into the river and twisted my leg on a rock."

"Poor dear." I fluffed up her pillows. "It looks terribly swollen."

I phoned room service for two buckets of ice and packed her leg with ice cubes and wet towels. "Does that feel better?"

"Oh, yes. Now I just need something for the pain."

The message was clear, and I poured her a tumblerful of Scotch.

"Whew!" Marilyn winced. "It burns! I've never taken it straight before." She took another large swallow, emptying the glass. After a moment, she said. "That's better. I don't feel a thing now." I just feel a little woozy." In minutes she was sound asleep, and I settled myself in a chair.

Later in the day a local doctor examined Marilyn's leg and told her she had a torn ligament. He advised her to stay off it for a couple of weeks, or otherwise there would be permanent damage. No sooner had the doctor left than DiMaggio phoned. He couldn't stay away from Marilyn any longer and had taken a room in a lodge at Lake Louise. "He'll be here in an hour!" Marilyn was beaming, looking as ecstatic as a little girl anticipating a dish of ice cream.

"Why doesn't he stay here with you?" I asked curiously.

She giggled. "You know Joe. He's such a fuddyduddy. He just won't risk the chance of any scandal."

I stood up and smiled at her. "Time to go, I'd say. Wouldn't you?"

"I would," she agreed happily. "But don't cross me off. Let's keep in touch. Okay?"

"Okay."

"I'm sorry," she said, holding out her arms, "I'm sorry we didn't have more time together."

"So am I." Now that I was about to leave, I didn't want to go. We held each other for a moment, then Marilyn kissed me quickly and softly on the lips. Looking up at me, she said, "Wish the best for me, Shutterbug."

I said I would. I went back to my room, packed, and phoned for a cab to take me to the airport.

A little later, when I boarded the plane, I could still taste the sweetness of Marilyn's lipstick on my lips. The welcoming stewardess noticed, and smiled. I felt foolish, and a little proud. I remember that as I took my seat my eyes were teary and I didn't give a damn whether the lipstick showed or not.

*Returning to Hollywood with Robert Mitchum after shooting*
River of No Return *in Banff, 1953.*

*"Soon I've got to face lawyers.... How I despise them—I distrust them all. They're the only crooks I know who never go to jail."*

$A$s always after a trip, I felt relieved to be back on Wallace Island, and my persona as an island man with island concerns—and a resort to run—took over. I wrote in my journal:

The first week of July brought many inquiries. Mr. Pichel wants to know the exact size of Wallace. Water temperature? Number of guests? Heat? Nearest doctors? Poison ivy? Is there a bridge? Golf? Maid service? What time is dinner served? The poor fellow! Wallace is not for him.

Then, later that summer—in August—came a note from Marilyn, the words scrawled in brown ink across lined paper.

Addressing me as usual as "Shutterbug," she advised me to brace myself— she'd said *yes* to Joe. He'd nearly fainted, spilling Scotch all over his pants. They were both very happy, Marilyn wrote, though they still quarreled a lot. Joe would get furious when she did sexy shots for photographers—almost like a wild bull. Often, she confessed, she'd get a naughty streak and pull up her skirt even farther just to irritate him. Joe was so old-fashioned and

77

*Times Square, 1980.*

stodgy; at times, she wrote, she thought he should have been a banker. But she immediately went on to say how kind and sweet and tender he was, how that made up for everything. Oh, how good it felt to be loved—protected—and adored!

Then she wrote about the next biggest event of her life, reminding me that she'd told me how as a little girl she used to go to the front of Grauman's Chinese Theatre and try to fit her feet into the cement imprints of all those great movie idols. Well, I was to brace myself again. That week, at the première of *Gentlemen Prefer Blondes,* along with Jane Russell she had pressed her hands and feet into the wet cement at Grauman's. Hey, wasn't that terrific! Now, she wrote triumphantly, she felt like a full-fledged movie star.

To my pleasure, the letter was signed with "much love."

Marilyn had passed a milestone, and in a few weeks so did I: Labor Day marked the end of our season.

> *Day after Labor Day.* How quiet! We feel like an occupied territory abandoned by a conquering army. The lawn chairs are empty, the boats lie idle, the wharf is bare of yachts. It is so still we can hear the pigeons devour the madrona berries. Davey [our son] is lost without playmates, and Wallie [the Conover dog] wanders hopefully from cottage to cottage looking for handouts. "We should be happy," Jeanne said. "We've got the island to ourselves again." But we aren't—not yet anyway.

Milestones for Marilyn were coming quickly now. In October she met the New York fashion photographer Milton Greene, who would have a profound effect on her screen career. Soon after they were introduced, they met again at a party given by Gene Kelly, where they retreated together from the noisy play of charades to a quiet corner and they struck an immediate rapport. Shortly afterwards, Marilyn wrote me a letter about her new acquaintance.

Like me, she said, Greene was a photographer. He was very sensitive and creative, with a boyish manner that hid a very worldly outlook. She was very excited about his ideas; the night before she wrote this to me, she had tossed for hours thinking about them. It was, she said, as if Greene could read her mind. He seemed to know instinctively the type of film Marilyn should do. She appreciated that he had guts, too—he wanted to liberate her from 20th Century-Fox and form their own film company, to be called Marilyn Monroe Productions. She was delighted by his enthusiasm, and just knew he was

78

*Jeanne and David Conover.*

*Wallace Island scenes.*

genuine. Of course, she pointed out, the only flaw was that Greene had had no motion picture experience. Yet Marilyn had faith in him: when she thought about it, she felt that the freshness of his approach to filmmaking could be just what her career needed. She was so happy—to think at last that she'd be able to play more serious roles, have script and director approval, not to mention what she called a "HUGE raise" in salary. Hey, wasn't that great?

Then she asked after me, telling me she thought of me often and wished I were with her to support her in these dealings. Joe, she wrote, wouldn't have anything to do with the film business, and soon she would have to face lawyers to draw up the papers. How she despised them, she declared—she distrusted them all. They were the only crooks she knew who never went to jail.

The rest of 1953 passed uneventfully. Perhaps, in spite of Marilyn, the year had been something of a disappointment to me. I find in my journal a sort of summing-up note:

> On looking back at this year's crop of guests, I find it disturbing that I can remember only a few. The majority leave no impression, no peculiarity that lingers, and fade quickly from memory. So many witless grins, limpid handshakes, pleasing overtures; so few faces that reflect clear-cut character. Sincerity, I fear, has succumbed to agreeableness. It's a trait that muddies the function of the best defined man. A solvent that levels down the human flesh.

But 1954 certainly began with a bang. A journal entry two weeks into the new year:

> *January 14.* Today the radio announced the marriage of Marilyn and Joe. I am pleased, yet apprehensive. The latter especially, since M. has so many reservations about their union. The closest unions are those of opposites, Goethe said. If this is true, M. and Joe are on safe ground. No two people could be more opposite. Joe is a very private person and resents any invasion of his privacy. M. is Miss Public herself. She loves people, parties, crowds, and the adulation of her fans. Joe is withdrawn and never says much. M. is outgoing and loves to talk. Joe is extremely jealous and possessive. Marilyn is neither particularly jealous nor possessive. Joe has a strong puritanical streak, but no one is less puritanical than M. The differences that probably separate them the most are that

neither one cares for the things the other cares most about—baseball and Hollywood. Now, Mr. Goethe, let's see how wise you are.

For months I heard nothing from Marilyn, and my journal deals solely with island life. It records a slightly testy exchange with Jeanne:

> *J.C.:* Let's get our facts straight. I told Mrs. Kirby the island was two miles long. You told her it was two and a half. Which is it?
> *D.C.:* Both—depends on the tide.

And an observation on our more frenetic guests:

> I am amused at how desperately Americans try to relax. After ten days, Morgan and Roberts are still going full blast. They've broken two badminton rackets, lost three fishing lines, wrecked a bicycle, and turned the horseshoe pits into bomb craters. For an American, it seems, the simplest thing is the hardest to do: nothing.

I missed Marilyn's phone calls and occasional notes, but I felt no news was good news. The newlyweds had leased a lovely Elizabethan cottage on North Palm Drive in Beverly Hills, and Marilyn was busy making *There's No Business Like Show Business.* She told everybody, including my brother, Austin, and Sidney Skolsky that she and her husband were very happy, although Joe never came to the studio and photographers were banned from taking pictures of the happy couple in their love nest. Knowing Joe's distaste for filmmaking and any kind of publicity, I gave no thought to that. Then, late in July, Austin wrote me, "I have seen Marilyn on two occasions, both at night on Sunset Strip, each time squired by a different man. Both times she looked unusually pale and bored; but last night at La Scala, with Hal Schaefer, she looked positively grim."

Was Goethe's axiom beginning to crumble?

In August Marilyn started filming *The Seven Year Itch* for Billy Wilder; Natasha Lytess was again by her side. Master of sophisticated comedy, Wilder was the perfect director for Marilyn at this time. He knew, as did everyone else, that all was not sweetness and light with the DiMaggios, and he was kind, endlessly patient and thoughtful. He didn't ask her why she came late or why she forgot her lines. He allowed her to go at her own pace, to do take after take. His air of nonchalance gave Marilyn comfort as well as confidence.

Wilder later said, "At no time did I find her malicious; mean, capricious, or anything but conscientious. There are certain urges and drives in her which make her different, but as a director, I think it's worth putting up with those things and living with them in order to work with her."

Early in September, when Marilyn was scheduled to finish the film on location in New York, she told Joe that Natasha would be accompanying them on the plane. Joe disliked anyone connected with the movie business, and no one more than Natasha, whose influence over Marilyn he resented bitterly. "If she goes," he declared, "I don't."

It was not an easy decision for Marilyn. Joe was plainly demanding that Marilyn choose between her career and their marriage.

She went to New York with Natasha.

Still, Joe's old-fashioned chivalry hung in. He drove her quietly—but tearfully—to the airport.

On the morning of October 3, much to no one's surprise, Marilyn and Joe announced their separation. A horde of reporters and curious onlookers was gathered outside the Elizabethan cottage. Marilyn's unquenchable thirst for publicity never left her, even during this, one of the saddest moments of her life. After DiMaggio's departure, she appeared before newsmen dressed all in black and fighting back tears, like a widow in mourning. For all the theatrics, though, I believe it was for her the death of a dream, the once bright hope she could make DiMaggio happy and still keep her career.

I couldn't get to sleep that night. I had the feeling Marilyn might call, which she often did when there was a crisis, or she needed someone close to talk to. So I got up and went into the kitchen and made a pot of coffee. It was eleven o'clock, far past my usual bedtime. I was worried about her, as I knew Marilyn would be heartbroken and all alone with only the phone to ease her distress. But I made it a point never to impinge on her privacy and nearly always left it to her to contact me. Shortly past midnight the radiophone buzzed. I picked up the mike.

"Hi. Have you heard the news?"

"Yes. I'm awfully sorry, Sweetheart."

"I tried so hard, really I did. Believe me. But I couldn't give up my career. I couldn't." Marilyn's voice was shrill with anguish.

"I thought Joe might meet you halfway."

"Oh, no. He's too pigheaded. If he bent a little he'd break."

"Then it's best if it's over."

*With Joe DiMaggio after their wedding, January 14, 1954.*

*Announcing their separation, October 3, 1954.*

*Joe DiMaggio at the funeral of Marilyn Monroe, August 8, 1962.*

"I know, I know," she cried. "But the trouble is I still love Joe. That's what makes it so hard. I feel terrible, I've treated him so beastly these last few weeks. Always working, never at home, too tired to cook and too busy studying my lines when I should have been giving him attention. I don't think he'll ever speak to me again."

"I'm sure he will." His good manners and honest concern for her, I thought, would see to that.

"I hope so. I'd hate to lose his friendship." She started crying.

"Listen, Sweetheart . . ." I racked my brain for something encouraging to say.

"Yeah."

"I know you feel lousy and the world right now looks pretty grim. But don't feel sorry for yourself. You've got to get on with your life. Get busy. Put all that negative energy into your work. It's the best antidote for pain. Surprise everybody with your resiliency. You've got the spunk. Okay?"

I heard a giggle. "Yes, Dr. Revonoc."

Two weeks later, Austin called. He sounded very excited: "Have I got news for you, kid. Wilder is in a state of shock. Marilyn arrives punctually at seven o'clock every morning. She knows her lines. She's easier to work with. She follows his direction and has never performed more brilliantly. And he can cut and print with only one or two takes. Isn't that something? Wilder said he had never seen such a drastic change in a person."

I was so pleased with the news I muttered aloud, "Thata girl, Sweetheart."

"What did you say?"

"Nothing. I just said you made my day."

Later that month at the divorce proceedings, Marilyn, still in black, began to sob as she testified. "I hoped to have out of my marriage love, warmth, affection, and understanding. But the relationship turned out to be one of coldness and indifference . . ." A few minutes later Judge Orlando H. Rhodes declared, "Divorce granted."

Marilyn was visibly shaken and teary-eyed as she left the courtroom. But fate was kind. In shedding a husband, she gained a close friend for life.

*"I just know I'm not happy unless I'm in love."*

I had to go to Los Angeles a few weeks later, and when my plane landed I went straight to a phone. I was concerned about Marilyn and eager to see her.

"Hi," she said excitedly. "Where are you?"

"At the airport."

"Good. Come on over."

I looked at my watch. It was 10:30 P.M. "Isn't it a little late?"

She laughed. "No, silly. You can stay here. I've got so much to tell you."

"Maybe tomorrow," I said. "You need your rest."

"Hey," came her whispery voice. "Stop worrying about me. I want to see you now. Really."

Marilyn was a difficult person to say no to, so I rented a car and drove to the house on North Palm Drive. She was waiting at the door, barefoot as usual, wearing a blue polka dot kimono. "Oh, Shutterbug," she squealed, flinging her arms around me, "it's so good to see you."

We kissed and hugged, then I held her at arms' length. "Say, I thought you'd be down in the dumps, but you look just great."

91

"I feel really great, too." Her eyes danced with life and her face glowed like a bright flower in the dimly lit room.

She filled two glasses with champagne and we sat on the sofa and looked at each other. She was even more beautiful than I remembered. "Okay," I said, feeling she had something important to tell me, "what's been happening?"

"I've quit Fox for good. I'm getting the hell out of Hollywood."

"Aren't you still under contract?"

"Nope. Not any longer. Greene's lawyer found a loophole. We're going to New York and put together Marilyn Monroe Productions. He's promised me fifty-one percent of the stock and a hundred thousand dollars a year salary. Plus I am the boss."

"Is that the only reason you're going?"

She blushed. "Oh, you know about Arthur?"

"Of course," I said. "You forget, I've got spies." She had met Arthur Miller several years before in Hollywood, and they had immediately taken a shine to each other; Austin kept me apprised of current developments.

She grinned. "Well, I can't go after him here when he lives in New York, can I?"

"It's that serious?"

"Yes."

The ink on her divorce papers was hardly dry. "Sure you aren't on the rebound?"

She looked at me with her innocent blue eyes. "I don't know. I just know I'm not happy unless I'm in love."

I smiled and shook my head. "I must say you aim high. Hollywood's loveliest actress and New York's greatest playwright. That's quite a combination."

"I think it'll work," she said, and sipped her drink. Then she put the glass down. "Arthur supports my career. He really believes I can be a dramatic actress. In fact, as soon as I get to New York, I'm going to enroll at Actors Studio. That is, if Lee Strasberg will take me."

"He'd be crazy if he didn't."

"I want to become a great actress. But I know it takes lots of work and study. Right now New York is the place to learn and the stage is the place to start. Greene is willing to pay all my expenses until the corporation gets underway. In fact, he and his wife, Amy, have invited me to stay with them."

"Won't that be a ticklish business?"

She shook her head. "I've got more confidence now. I think I can handle it. Besides, Amy is very sophisticated and self-assured. I don't think she'll feel threatened."

"Propinquity leads to indiscretion," I warned. "What if you fall in love with Greene?"

She shook her head slowly. "He's much too boyish. I like older men. You know, a father figure. Someone I can lean on as well as look up to."

The description, of course, sounded like DiMaggio. "Have you seen Joe since the divorce?"

"Oh, yes." Her eyes brightened. "He brought me flowers and visited me often when I was in the hospital for surgery. We'll always be good friends."

"That's good. Some people make better friends than husbands."

"I think you're right." Marilyn took a large swallow of champagne, then, as she often did, changed the subject abruptly. "Hey, you never told me what you did during the war. Weren't you in the Philippines?"

"Yes."

"Well, what happened? Did you win any medals?"

I could feel my face flush. "No, not exactly. I was a librarian."

"That fits." She giggled. "It must have been very boring."

"Oh, no. Not at all. I had a very attractive staff. They were delightfully uninhibited."

Marilyn snuggled against me and ran her fingers through my hair. "Go on, tell me more. You've got me all excited."

I look at my watch. It was nearly 2 A.M. "Perhaps some other time. I'm really tired."

Her eyes, sultry now, gazed at me. "Shall we hit the sack?"

I didn't know whether she meant separately or together, but I knew what I meant to do. "I'll sleep here on the sofa. That'll be fine."

"You don't need to," she purred. "My bed is much more comfortable."

"No. The sofa is okay."

She looked hurt. "You mean you don't want to go to bed with me?"

"I didn't say that. I just said that I'd like to sleep on the sofa." I didn't want her to feel I was refusing her, because I did want to have sex with her; even the thought was exciting. But something told me, Don't let your body control your mind. Hands off . . . this could be dynamite.

"Why?" she asked.

"I'm just not sure it's a good idea for us to go to bed together."

"I don't understand. We've been to bed with each other before. Why not now?"

"It's different now," I said. I still held the old-fashioned idea that sex involved commitment, particularly if you cared very much for the party involved.

"What's so different about it? You're being so strange. What are you trying to say?"

I told her the truth. "It would be nice to go to bed with you, believe me. But I just think it's best now to keep our relationship platonic. Sex would complicate things."

She burst out laughing. "Oh, Shutterbug, you're such a funny man. How in the world would our going to bed together complicate our relationship?"

I had to think how to put it into words, and I finally put it rather clumsily. "Listen, I don't want you to feel I'm after anything. Because I'm not. But when two people become lovers they soon stop being friends. That is, friends like before. The quality of their relationship changes. They expect more of each other, are able to make more demands of one another. There's a loss of independence and freedom."

"But that won't happen. We live miles apart and only see each other rarely. Besides, I plan to marry Arthur."

"Well, let's look at it from a different angle. Suppose we did go to bed together, and we had fun. Then some morning after I'm gone you'll wake up and say to yourself, 'You know, that guy only came to see me to get some sex. How could he do that? He used me.' "

"You aren't like that."

"I know. But you could begin to think that way if I began to visit you more often." I finished my drink. "Now let's say we went to bed and for you the sex is lousy. Would you really want to see me again? And if you did, wouldn't you feel uncomfortable?"

"Yes. But you're a good bedmate."

"Perhaps, way back. But for you things might have changed since then. Undoubtedly you've had a lot of lovers. Also, a husband. Right?"

She nodded, an amused smile on her face.

"Your expectations would have grown immensely. I doubt if I could live up to them."

"It's worth a try, isn't it?"

"Is it worth risking our relationship? It's doubtful it would ever be the same."

She paused. "I never thought about it that way. I'm beginning to see what you mean."

She got up and went to the linen closet and brought me a blanket. "Goodnight, Shutterbug," she said, kissing my cheek.

"Goodnight, Sweetheart."

She disappeared into the bedroom. A moment later she peeked out the door. "Hey, you know something?"

"No."

"You're a nut. But I love you."

There's No Business Like Show Business, *1954*.

*"Like you said, to become somebody,
you have to BE somebody."*


*I*n 1955 I was working on the book that became *Once Upon an
Island,* and finding more time to write. This activity puzzled
Davey, and I noted this overheard conversation in my journal:

"Why does Papa go to his den?" Davey asked his mother.
"To work, dear. He's writing a book."
"Why?"
"Because he wants to."
"Why does he want to, Mom? We've got so many."

Television had come to Wallace Island, and in March I watched Marilyn
on Edward R. Murrow's *Person to Person.* The telecast, from the Weston,
Connecticut, country house of Milton and Amy Greene, did not come off
well for Marilyn. During the interview she sat tongue-tied before the camera,
like a shy and dreamy high school kid, while Amy Greene fielded most of
her questions.

I felt embarrassed for her, and a little sad. Amy Greene had stolen the show—or so I thought until Jeanne remarked, "My God, she's such a fragile and helpless thing, you want to cuddle and protect her like a kitten." In fifteen minutes, Marilyn had succeeded in winning over one of her bitterest critics: my wife. "She's got a lot more than sex appeal," Jeanne said. "She has sweetness, warmth, and lovableness. No wonder you were captivated by her."

But watching that show was my only "contact" with Marilyn for some months, and I was more and more settled in my island life.

> For weeks now I have had no inclination to leave the island. If I don't watch out, I'll soon take root like a fir. The prospect, I admit, I find not unpleasant.

In June, Marilyn wrote from New York. She said she was on a learning spree—out after everything that would enrich her. She was determined that her life should have more value. She remembered what I'd once told her, that to become somebody, you've got to BE somebody. She said she didn't care what people said, she wanted to be a serious artist, and that Lee Strasberg thought she could be. His ideas, she felt, were exciting, and she described them to me: that he related acting to your life in a way that you can use your past on stage; he called it "emotional memory." That was why, she explained, he recommended psychoanalysis, so one could discover and utilize the deep feeling hidden in our inner selves. I wasn't so sure, and I noted:

> I'm afraid analysis will do Marilyn more harm than good. It will be like opening Pandora's Box, releasing all the ugliness and misery of her childhood that her conscious wishes to forget. The result could lead to deterioration of the psyche, the undermining of an ego that has been steadfastly built with much pain in the hostile world of Hollywood.

Overall, the year 1955 in New York was one of the happiest of Marilyn's life. She had formed her own film production company with Milton Greene, enjoyed the Actors Studio and her classes with Lee Strasberg, and had fallen more deeply in love with Arthur Miller. (Joe, for the moment, was out of the picture. In a phone call around this time, she told me that Joe had tried to get back in her life by taking her to the première of *The Seven Year Itch*, but all they did was argue. "Joe is such a fuddyduddy," she said. "He just doesn't fit into my life.")

"It seems half my problems disappear when I'm in love," she told me. "I have more time to think—and to give. I feel more eager to learn and enjoy. I get up early, yearning for Arthur to call. When he does, my heart races. I can barely utter a word. Warm all over with happiness."

Marilyn had a way of making all men feel she could be in love with them: conscious or not, it was a sort of protective device by which she saved up each one for the rainy day when she needed help or attention.

She loved New York. It offered her independence and freedom. She could blend into the crowds, unnoticed, and not have to wear fancy clothes or makeup. Every day was her own to do as she wished. She slept late; she went shopping and to parties; she began seeing an analyst; she made friends in the legitimate theatre. She met the famous directors Elia Kazan and Joshua Logan; Logan would direct her in *Bus Stop* and become one of her most ardent supporters. She loved meeting eminent people and the company of actors and intellectuals. Such people increased her thirst for knowledge. She browsed in bookstores as well as in Saks, caring for what went into her head as well as what covered her body. Of course, she always had: years before, unlike any other Hollywood starlet she had opened her first charge account not at I. Magnin's but at Marian Hunter's Bookshop.

Marilyn rarely missed a session at the Actors Studio. She signed in like everyone else and sat quietly in the back of the class so she could not be seen. Wearing a baggy sweater, jeans or slacks, and no makeup, her platinum hair covered by a kerchief, she blended in with the rest of the students, unnoticed and unbothered. Here she was student, not star, and she saw herself that way; when she called another student about working on a scene together, she introduced herself simply and unselfconsciously: "Hi—it's Marilyn—from class."

Marilyn worried about her nervousness, which at times made her stutter. "Nervousness, for an actress," Strasberg said, putting her at ease, "is not a handicap. It's a sign of sensitivity." All she had to do was to channel this excess energy into her work.

At each session members performed short scenes, and then they critically discussed their performances. A reverential hush would follow as Strasberg himself analyzed their work. For Marilyn, Actors Studio was a big family, with Strasberg the strict patriarch (and priest and psychiatrist as well). His wife, Paula, herself a drama coach, became her closest friend. Marilyn felt at ease and safe. The Strasbergs reinforced her belief in herself, helped her to improve her talent, and saw in her the potential greatness of a serious

*With Robert F. Wagner, Mayor of New York, 1955.*

actress. She was enraptured. All this was more than she had hoped for, and she was determined not to disappoint them.

I was glad Marilyn seemed so well and happy; that summer was not an easy one at Wallace Island.

> Tinder dry. No rain has fallen since May; the grass is burnt brown except under the apple trees, and the garden withers. Danger of fire worries us.
> "How's the water?" Jeanne asked while collecting the shriveled string-beans.
> "Not good," I said. "I've had to cut back the toilets. The well is dropping fast."

But there were, as always, consolations:

> This morning I overheard Mrs. Barnes, while sitting on the edge of the sandbox, ask Davey, "What do you like to do best, dear?"
> "Fishin'."
> "Second best?"
> He thought for a moment. "Fishin' with Papa."

When Marilyn phoned me in July, she said, "New York is my home now. I'll make pictures in Hollywood, but I won't live there. I am a serious actress. I want to do stage plays here on Broadway." There were both determination and confidence in her voice.

"Are you still seeing Miller?" I asked.

"Yes, often. We meet secretly, usually at his friends the Rostens'."

"Why secretly?"

"He doesn't want to embarrass his wife."

This sounded like a lame excuse; certainly, it wasn't the real reason. Miller was all but separated from his wife and maintained a private social life. "He could get an apartment," I said. "It would be easier on you both."

"He's too frugal," Marilyn said uneasily.

I thought it best to drop the subject. I tried another, hoping to bring out her fighting spirit. "They're saying Hollywood is washed up with you. That you'll never be able to make another film there."

She laughed. "Rubbish! By the end of the year Fox will beg for my return. I'll be able to call the shots. Wait and see."

"That's my Marilyn—spunky as all hell." And I hoped with all my heart that she was right. I couldn't see her making an eight-forty curtain every night.

Fortunately, Marilyn's prediction came true. The top brass at Fox missed the tremendous income she brought in, and became suitors. Finally, on December 31, they offered her a new contract, giving her $100,000 per film and the right to choose script, director, and cameraman, as well as other concessions no movie star had obtained before. She could not refuse. Marilyn Monroe Productions had been on the verge of bankruptcy; she had pulled off a cunning gamble.

As the year ended, Marilyn's career was being managed by a heady triumvirate: Greene, Miller, and Strasberg. Each of these artists was devoted to her and eager to develop her talent. What power she wielded over their lives! It was a little like three Sir Walter Raleighs throwing their cloaks over the mud puddle for Good Queen Bess. How Marilyn must have enjoyed watching them all compete for her attention and commendation!

"This arrangement won't last," I wrote in my journal, "even if each one seeks sincerely to bring out the best in her. I suspect the photographer will be the first to go."

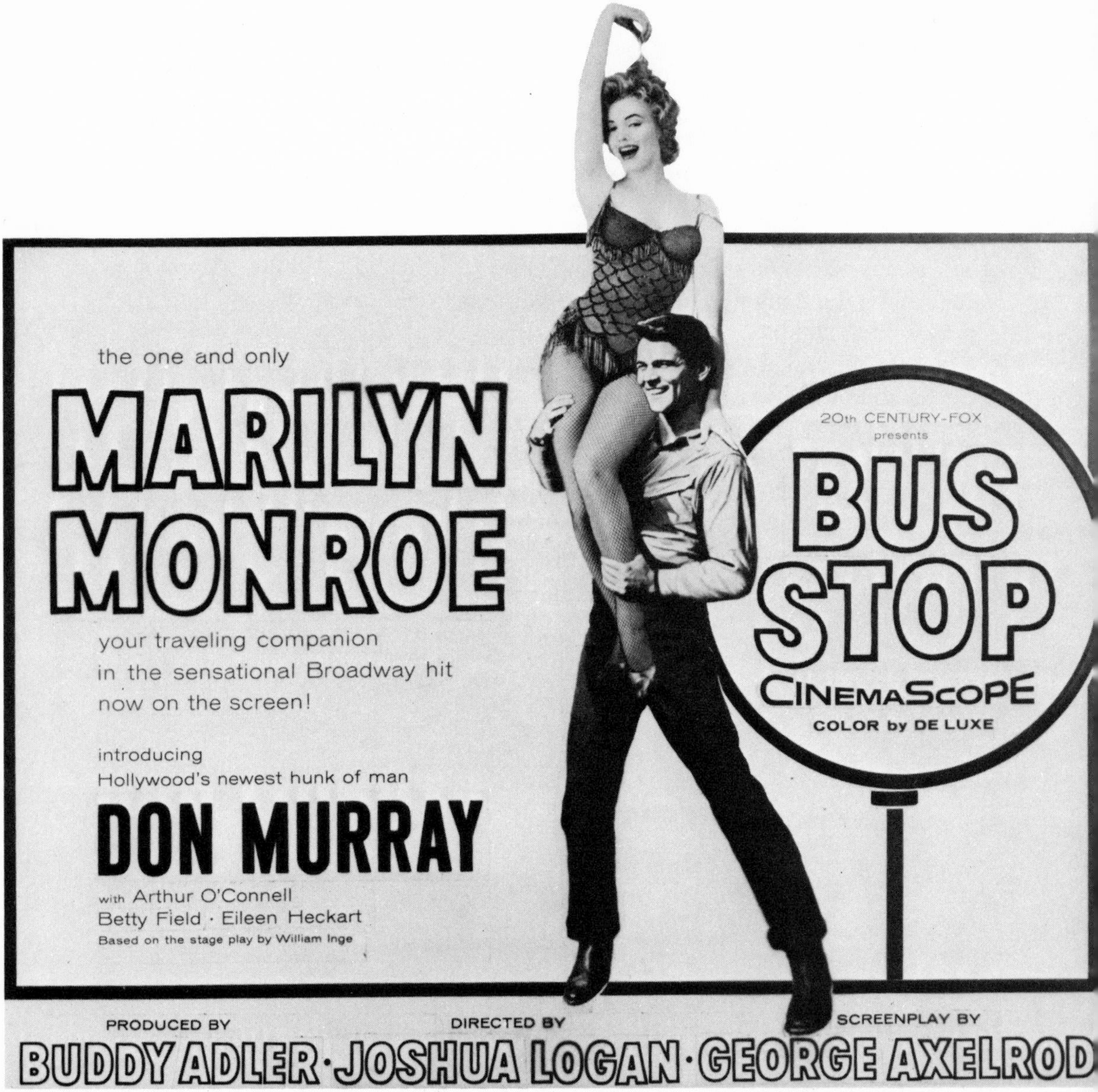

the one and only

# MARILYN MONROE

your traveling companion
in the sensational Broadway hit
now on the screen!

introducing
Hollywood's newest hunk of man

## DON MURRAY

with Arthur O'Connell
Betty Field · Eileen Heckart
Based on the stage play by William Inge

20th CENTURY-FOX
presents

# BUS STOP

### CINEMASCOPE

COLOR by DE LUXE

PRODUCED BY          DIRECTED BY          SCREENPLAY BY

## BUDDY ADLER · JOSHUA LOGAN · GEORGE AXELROD

*"Why haven't I the right to grow and
expand like everybody else?"*

For Marilyn, 1956 started out filled with promise. In January Greene signed a contract with Fox for Marilyn to do *Bus Stop;* Joshua Logan would direct. Miller finally left his wife in readiness to obtain a divorce in Reno. At the Actors Studio, Marilyn delivered a stunning performance as Anna in a scene from Eugene O'Neill's *Anna Christie* that moved her remote and magisterial teacher almost to tears. Then, at a press conference on February 9, she announced the capture of Sir Laurence Olivier for her leading man in her own production of *The Prince and the Showgirl.* Before the two hundred reporters gathered in the Plaza Hotel, she was radiant, excited, and obviously very pleased to be appearing arm in arm with the great British actor. Gone was the dumb blonde, the shy high school kid. The public would now take her seriously. This was the cleverest coup of her career, good not only for her prestige but also for her self-confidence—with the added bonus, perhaps, of the hope that some of his talent would rub off on her.

But the press conference was a disaster. Marilyn had not kept her fences mended where it counted most. In New York these past few months she had

105

isolated herself from the press. She had refused to grant interviews or answer questions about her relationship with Miller, and her aloofness bred hostility in the news media. Now the reporters, pushing Olivier out of the way, turned on her like a pack of dogs. She was asked embarrassing questions, which she answered with simple dignity and honesty. In a sudden frenzy they surged around her, shouting brutal questions, until she and her press agent were forced against the wall. Then Marilyn employed an ingenious tactic, breaking a strap on her low-cut black satin dress. The room gasped in awe. A safety pin was found, the "damage" repaired—and Marilyn spun around on her high-heeled pumps and left the room, vice president Greene trailing in her wake.

After a fourteen-month absence, Marilyn's return to Hollywood for *Bus Stop* in February was triumphant. The airport was besieged with thousands of admirers and reporters; it took her two hours to get through the crowd. She was acclaimed like a queen restored to her throne. And indeed there was now something regal about her, the way she held her head, the sureness of her walk, the confident sparkle in her eyes. "I don't envy those big boys at Fox," my brother wrote to me. "Marilyn's got power now. Treated as a hireling for so many years, she's going to have her own way. And it's high time."

On Marilyn's struggle upward, she had been forced to conceal her nature under a simple demeanor of humility. This guise of purity and innocence was not strange to her. During her childhood she had used it effectively, though unconsciously, to win love and favor in her succession of foster homes. Later, Aunt Ana reinforced this behavior by inoculating Norma Jean against reality with her own religious belief that the external world is merely what you believe it to be in your own mind. This was "a dangerously seductive philosophy," as Alexander Walker observed in his admirable book, *The Celluloid Sacrifice*, "for actors whose sense of reality is often impaired by the illusions they live among and project in their performances." This probably accounts "for the beguilingly dreamy way in which Monroe moved through her films—and life—oblivious to any menacing element in her environment." And yet it was this innocence that made her luminous. The glow was not tarnished by either ugliness or the harshness of her experiences. In fact, it even grew brighter—almost ethereal—towards the close of her life, as can be seen in shots from the unfinished *Something's Got to Give*. The invincibility of her spirit remained constant to the end.

In many respects, Marilyn was a "natural" actress whose most enduring

*With Milton Greene at an airport press conference on her return to Hollywood, February 25, 1956.*

love affair was with the still camera. She knew instinctively how to pose, how to convey sadness or joy, love or contempt, with the slightest facial expression or the fewest words. She knew that her charm, more than her shape, was the real source of her magic and power.

Marilyn's magic stemmed partly from her Gemini makeup. She was able to alter her personality to fit the role required of her, which is why so many people saw her so differently. With almost every man she found an element of identification that corresponded to his own interests and needs. As an actress, she was able to make this same identification with each and every moviegoer, and that I believe is the ultimate secret of her triumph on the screen.

Now queen of her own production company, pretense for political reasons was no longer necessary. Marilyn could be her own person. The months in New York had prepared her well. She had become more knowledgeable and, through effort and study, had succeeded in widening the scope of her artistry. Analysis with Dr. Marianne Kris and Strasberg's teaching had made her freer of inhibition and moral sanction, and she was now able to speak her mind. Instead of repressing hostility, which resulted in psychosomatic illness, she could vent it openly. Her sexuality had increased. She looked more in command of herself, more sophisticated, and she dressed with more style. She had class, poise, self-assurance. She was the "new" Marilyn Monroe.

Still, the public and the press had taken a skeptical view of her desire to become a serious actress. A book appeared whose title asked, *Will Acting Spoil Marilyn Monroe?* She was baffled and sometimes hurt by those who sought to keep her the dumb blonde. "Why haven't I the right to grow and expand like everyone else?" she demanded in a phone call to me.

In the face of the evidence, nobody believed that anyone as beautiful as Marilyn could have any brains: her witticisms were declared to be the work of her press agents. But she stood up bravely to her tormentors, as one press woman could certainly attest. The reporter asked Marilyn snidely, "How long can a whale stay under water?"

Disgusted, Marilyn replied, "Why do you ask me such a question?"

"It's kind of an intelligence test."

Marilyn shot back, "Yours or mine?"

In the filming of *Bus Stop*, Marilyn was determined to prove to everyone she could act. With Paula Strasberg as her new coach, she never worked harder, or more seriously—and with Greene supervising her makeup, she never looked more entrancing.

*With Don Murray on the set of* Bus Stop, *1956.*

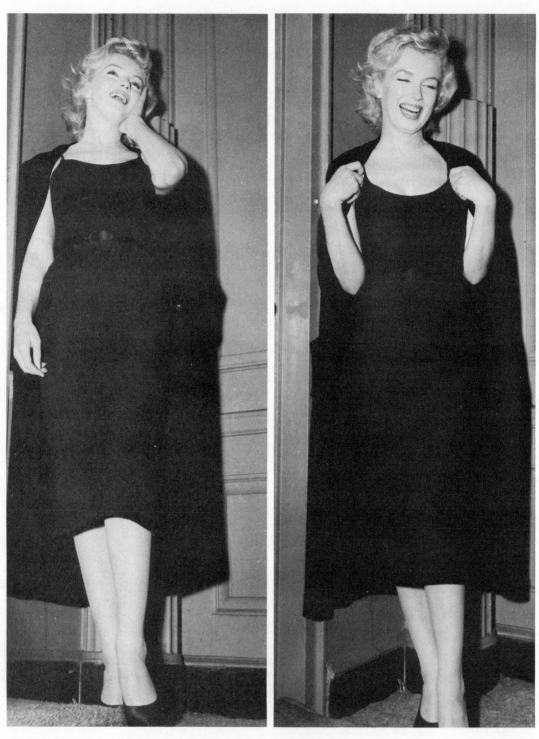

*Announcing her engagement to Arthur Miller, June 21, 1956.*

Joshua Logan, who was initially skeptical of her acting talent, grew more impressed each day. "I was beginning to feel," he later said almost in an apology, "that she had always been brilliant." In the role of Cherie, Marilyn had achieved perfection as a tragicomedian, as only Chaplin and, at times, Garbo, had done before her.

*Bus Stop* was well received by the press. But what pleased Marilyn the most were Joshua Logan's words when he was interviewed by Maurice Zolotow: "Monroe is as near a genius as any actress I ever knew. . . . She is the most completely realized and authentic film actress since Garbo. . . . Watch her work. In any film. How rarely she has to use words. How much she does with her eyes, her lips, with slight, almost accidental gestures. . . . Monroe is pure cinema."

Despite her performance in *Bus Stop*, the public could not be altogether convinced of her talent, anymore than they could take seriously her relationship with Arthur Miller. But serious it was.

*June 21.* Marilyn and Miller's wedding announcement came out today in the most unusual and startling manner—in the U.S. Congress. I find it most disconcerting that Miller would drag in Marilyn's name to obtain a U.S. passport. However, I am sure they are both very much in love, and M. herself, being an expert publicist, might have devised the scheme. I suspect they both have selfish motives for the union. M. seeks respect more than anything else, and Miller has it by the carload. He is also a father figure; his face even resembles Abraham Lincoln— Marilyn's favorite hero. As for Miller, undoubtedly he seeks to fill a void in his life, and what better way to fill it than with the most desired woman in the world. Also, M. has money. I have grave doubts it will work. How do you feel about the plunge, I asked M. on the phone. Really great, she said with not too much enthusiasm. I'm going to try my best to make it work. We are so happy, it's unbelievable. Wish the best for me, Shutterbug. I promised I would.

Later, she expressed her doubt more visibly when she wrote on the back of her wedding picture, "Hope, hope, hope."

*"I am so confused and miserable—*
*I don't know what to do—"*

Just before Marilyn's marriage to Arthur Miller in a civil ceremony on June 29, 1956, the happy couple held a meeting for the press on the grounds of Miller's house in Roxbury, Connecticut. An army of reporters and photographers was gathered on the lawn. When Marilyn and Miller stepped out the door, they were mobbed. It was chaos, a rerun of the press conference at the Plaza. This time Milton Greene stepped in and restored order by scheduling the reporters into time slots. Miller looked as if he were in a state of shock, his granite face sheet-white. This was his first taste of what it would be like being married to a movie star, and his behavior was much the same as DiMaggio's had been. For an hour the couple was grilled by newsmen and shouted at by photographers. "Put your arm around him!" "Stand over here!" "Look over there!" "Hold it!" "Hey, Arthur, can't you smile?" This last was a refrain that would be heard throughout their marriage.

Two days later, a religious ceremony performed by Rabbi Robert Goldberg was held at the home of friends of Miller's. Marilyn, radiating her inner joy, looked lovely and serene in her simple wedding outfit; she would never again know such happiness.

113

*With Laurence Olivier in* The Prince and the Showgirl, *1956.*

Soon afterwards, Marilyn was asked by Zolotow if Miller would play a role in her film company. "Oh, no," she said. "Absolutely not. My company, well, that's my business. My husband is pleasure."

After the wedding the Greenes and Strasbergs in tow, the Millers flew to England, where Marilyn began filming *The Prince and the Showgirl*. She never felt secure without an entourage of faithful workers and coaches, secretaries and press agents. She needed constant support in her work in order to function. Now that she had a husband, some of the burden of providing that support would fall on Arthur's shoulders.

At the London airport, the Millers were greeted by Sir Laurence and his wife, Vivien Leigh; also present was a wild mob of reporters, movie fans, and curious onlookers. Bedlam ensued. Photographers trampled on each other, a newsreel camera smashed to the ground, a photographer had to be rushed to the hospital with crushed hands and feet.

Miss Leigh was aghast. "Are all your receptions like this?"

"Well, no." Marilyn grinned. "This one is a little more restrained than usual."

At a formal reception a little later at the Savoy Hotel, the British press was considerably less restrained with their questions. At first, Marilyn fielded them handily.

"Are you really studying acting?"

"Yes."

"What inspired you to study acting?"

"Seeing my own films," she replied, smiling.

Applause. Then someone in the back shouted, "What are your tastes in music?"

"Hmm, let me see. Well, jazz, like Louis Armstrong, you know, and Beethoven."

"Oh, Beethoven? What Beethoven numbers in particular, Miss Monroe?"

The audience waited. Marilyn bit her lip. "I have a terrible time with numbers," she mumbled finally, "but I know it when I hear it."

It got worse. "What is your definition of an intellectual?"

It was a clear slap at her integrity and at her marriage, and it was more than Marilyn could stand. "Oh, go look it up in the dictionary," she snapped.

Marilyn's humiliations at the hands of the press were not limited to such treatment. Stories were fabricated by reporters. A newsman met her one day, carrying under her arm a copy of Keats's letters, which I had sent her and knew she adored. He asked: "Are you a Keats fan?" Her supposed reply:

*July 1, 1956.*

"I don't know . . . it's just the right weight to balance on my head to learn to walk right." I'm sure she said no such thing.

In my journal that June, I wrote:

> In England, M. has not been received well by the press. The vicious attacks by reporters must be hard for her to understand, since the English are known for their civility and good manners. One can only say, Sweetheart, the ways of man are weird and enigmatic. As soon as they create something beautiful, they seek ways to destroy it. Of the seven original wonders of the world, how many survive today?

In July came a postcard from Egham, where she and Miller had rented a large house on an estate near Windsor. Compared to California, she wrote, England seemed tiny and quaint with its little toy trains chugging through the miniature countryside. Work with Olivier was apparently not going smoothly: she said that Sir L. and she clashed a lot, that he was arrogant and demanding. Marilyn told me he had no feelings—that she got better response from a gas station attendant. But she was philosophical, saying that oh, well, it kept Arthur busy, that he was mending the conflicts.

I watched with keen interest the reports in the press of the battles that were taking place at Pinewood Studios. Olivier had been warned by Logan to be kind and patient with Marilyn, to keep his voice down, not to expect her to leap into the role at his command. It took time for her to get into the mood of the character, to achieve spontaneity. Director-actor Olivier had no such frivolous notions of acting. You arrived on the set with your homework done. Period.

When shooting had hardly started, he exclaimed, "All right, Marilyn. Be sexy!" Marilyn was furious and humiliated. She was not a machine. Sex was not something you could turn on and off like a coffee pot. She fled to her dressing room and called Strasberg at his London hotel. "Lee, how do you become sexy? What do you do to be sexy?" But Strasberg had no answers she could use.

The press stated that Olivier was having trouble with Marilyn. Strasberg stated that Marilyn was having trouble with Olivier. Marilyn retreated into sickness and pills. She could not sleep and arrived late on the set. She was groggy from the quantities of Nembutal and codeine she took to ease unendurable menstrual pain. She mumbled her lines, she forgot her lines. She lost her temper. She shrieked at everybody.

Near the end of August, I had a letter from her. She was miserably unhappy.

She had, she wrote, seen Arthur's notebook lying on a table in their house, open to a page on which she'd read the following words: "Why do you like to hurt me if you love me? I thought you were an angel, but Mary [Miller's first wife] was a saint compared to you. Olivier is right. You are a troublesome bitch. What a waste of love! All you want is a flunky. Someone who'll make excuses for you, to wait on you night and day, pour out sweet talk to make you feel better and wake you up from the stupor of pills. Well, I'm not up to it. Damn it, I'm not your servant. I'll not bow my head again. Never! You've made love a drudgery. The only one I really love in this world is my daughter."

Marilyn was shocked, and deeply hurt. How, she demanded, could he say such dreadful things? She'd been sick for days, she wrote, and under tremendous strain. What had Miller expected when he'd married her—a picnic? Besides, Marilyn pointed out, he had chosen to play peacemaker between her and "Mister Sir," as she called Olivier, although time after time she had told him he didn't need to get involved, that it was none of his business. She railed against Miller, that he'd had to poke his nose into her affairs, saying they'd lose money if she didn't arrive on the set on time. If he misplaced a dime, she said, that was a catastrophe. She was so confused and miserable, she wrote. She didn't know what to do.

Poor Marilyn, I thought. What a time she has with husbands. I wrote in my journal,

> DiMaggio hated her career and everything to do with it; now Miller is supportive, but unable to cope with Marilyn's film work. Or is it her unstable temperament? Yet, Arthur's anger smacks more of self-pity, anger at himself as much as at her. It sounds more like the whine of a man who cannot accept the humble aspects of his wedding vows. One does not ordinarily, in two months of marriage, run dry of compassion. In light of his extreme self-centeredness, it is only fair to speculate if Miller was ever in love. Since he seems to have the hardheartedness of the intellectual and a Simon Legree's grasp for money, his sincerity is questionable. He is also overtly ambitious, perhaps at this point more ambitious than M. It will not surprise me any day to hear that Miller has pushed Greene out and taken over the custodianship of her career.

And indeed, Miller now stepped into the ring of Marilyn's career, ready to take over Greene's duties. He would not share either his wife or her money much longer.

Soon after, Miller rushed back to the States. His daughter was ill, and he expected to stay with her a couple of weeks. Marilyn was distraught. She became ill, so emotionally disturbed that she could not work. Miller returned quickly to Marilyn's side, and the following day she went back to work. I had to wonder if, for Miller, it was the pull of love, or fear over the continued loss of money. In any case, the notebook crisis had passed; it was not spoken of again. But like a smoldering fire in Marilyn's conscious, it was not altogether out.

When filming of *The Prince and the Showgirl* had stumbled to an end, Marilyn spoke to the cast and apologized for having been "so nasty" to everyone. "I hope you will all forgive me. It wasn't my fault. I've been very sick all through the picture. Please—please don't hold it against me." Few stars of her magnitude have ever felt the need to apologize for their behavior. But Marilyn was not afraid to be human, and in every role she played, people could see and feel her humanity on the screen. They could see her fragility, her vulnerability and helplessness, her yearning to be loved.

When the Millers left England in the fall, they hardly spoke to Greene. Marilyn and Arthur's relationship had the making of a new life. But I believe it was not so much a deepening of love as recognition of their common plight. They needed each other.

*"I am pregnant again....God knows
I should be happy, but I'm <u>not.</u>
I'm depressed....Oh, how I want
the child—but now I don't.
Not really, not deep down."*

Soon after the Millers' arrival in New York, Paula Strasberg told a newspaper interviewer, "I have never seen such tenderness and love as Arthur and Marilyn feel for each other. How he values her! I don't think any woman I've ever known has been so *valued* by a man."

Early in the new year, Marilyn discovered she was pregnant. To have a child was one of her fondest dreams. She was radiantly happy, as the photos of her and Miller frolicking on the beach at Amagansett, Long Island, so explicitly show. The couple bought a farm in Roxbury, Connecticut, and settled into an informal life of domestic bliss. Unhappily, during her sixth week of pregnancy Marilyn miscarried and the dream was shattered. She sank into a period of depression, almost of hopelessness. Large quantities of Nembutals failed to make life tolerable. To cheer her, Miller announced that he would write a movie script for her from a short story he had written, *The Misfits*.

This picked up her spirits decidedly. She had always thought Miller would write for her someday, although it was against his principles to create a character with someone in mind. For a while she became her old self again.

*With Tony Curtis and Jack Lemmon in* Some Like It Hot, *1959.*

She played with their basset hound, Hugo, baked bread, weeded the garden, and went into the village shopping, while her husband labored at the type-writer. But country life began to bore her. "It's the constant sameness every day," she complained. The restless Gemini needed change.

So the Millers rented a thirteenth-floor apartment at 444 East 57th Street in New York with a lovely view over the East River. Marilyn started classes with Strasberg again at the Actors Studio, and the work with other students there gave her a feeling of belonging. Her mind was much on her career. She could hardly wait to see the first draft of *The Misfits*. Her respect for Miller had grown considerably, yet deep inside she wondered whether he was writing the screenplay as an expression of his love for her, or simply to use her as a means of regaining his prestige as a playwright. She was haunted perpetually by the fear of being used, and the notebook affair was never far below the surface. Suspicions plunged Marilyn into deep depressions that were a mystery both to her husband and to friends like Norman and Hedda Rosten. These avalanches of gloom worked to make sleep impossible, to undermine her psyche, and to rouse again the fear of insanity.

In February, at Miller's urging, Marilyn cast Greene adrift. She had no heart for it, she told me later. "In the lawyer's office, I couldn't face him. I just broke and ran out the door. After all, he was responsible for the two best pictures I've ever made."

"Why did you give in to Arthur, then?"

"He was always hounding me. I couldn't stand it anymore. Besides, *The Misfits* was to be a joint effort. We had to work together closely. I felt, you know, I had to keep peace."

When Marilyn bought out Greene's interest in Marilyn Monroe Productions, the Millers were left with little money. Though her income was considerable, Marilyn was not a lavish spender. But she was a lavish giver. She could never say no to a friend, or to charity performances. Even when she was unknown and broke, Marilyn had given her old Pontiac to her dramatic coach, Natasha Lytess, and took buses herself. Many times in her life she gave away nearly everything she owned.

Unlike most movie stars, Marilyn had no desire for expensive possessions. She was unimpressed by fancy cars, dazzling jewelry, palatial mansions, or lavish wardrobes. I remember getting her coat for her once and being amazed at the sparseness of her closet. "You've got a lot more books than you have clothes," I exclaimed. "It's my mind that needs the help," she replied, laughing.

What Marilyn saved on luxury items she spent on cosmetics, perfume, and hairdressers, as well as on maintaining various residences. Her one real extravagance was the telephone; she admitted that one month her bill amounted to a thousand dollars. The telephone was the one friend she could count on when she was lonely or upset or when she needed advice. "Besides,". she reasoned, "it's easier to talk than write letters."

Marilyn's checkbook was always open. She was forever writing checks to people she felt needed money, particularly the Strasbergs, to whom she gave large sums for their services as well as donations to the Studio. In fact, she was extremely generous to everybody except herself. She once remarked candidly, "I don't care about money. I just want to be wonderful."

Near the end of July 1958 she was back at her favorite stomping ground, the Beverly Hills Hotel, ready to shoot *Some Like It Hot* for Billy Wilder. Paula Strasberg and, reluctantly, Arthur Miller were at her side. Every picture of Marilyn's was a burden for him. Along with her protective army of staff, she needed his constant reassurances, his love and attention. Despite her growing sophistication, she had no inner resources to counteract her fear that she wouldn't be able to perform well enough. She had no confidence in her ability. Her ever increasing reliance on people she felt she could trust must have placed an almost unbearable weight on Miller's shoulders. To be with her constantly, supporting her, all day, every day—and sometimes all through the night—was an untenable position even for a saint. No marriage could go on this way.

When she was working, Marilyn was not really suited for marriage. Her career now dominated her life so completely there was little room for her to accommodate a satisfactory personal relationship. She was a perfectionist, and the devotion she gave to her art was absolute. She studied for hours, even days, to perfect a segment that lasted only two minutes on film. She worked harder than any other player on the set, and the strain eroded her precarious emotional balance and drew out all her bitchiness. Yet, when the film reached the screen, she presented a picture of such tenderness, innocence, and sweet wistfulness that it took one's breath away. Her gift and genius were strictly her own, which prompted Wilder to say of Marilyn, "There has never been a woman with such voltage on the screen with the exception of Garbo." Still, he wasn't prepared for the host of difficulties Marilyn would present him.

Often a visitor on the set of *Some Like It Hot*, Austin wrote, "Marilyn's behavior is worse than ever. She's not only consistently late, but she can't

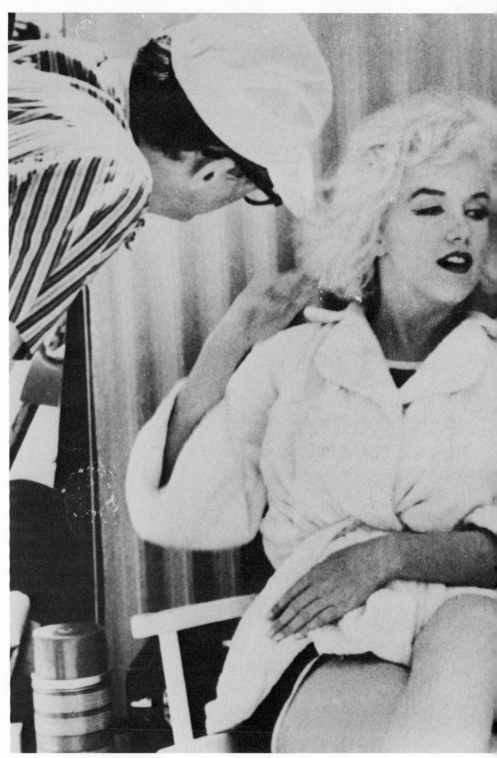

*With Arthur Miller and Paula Strasberg on location for*
Some Like It Hot, *1959.*

remember the simplest lines. She blows scene after scene. She demands too many takes—sometimes thirty or forty—which exhausts the players opposite her and stretches Wilder's patience beyond endurance. I've never seen her so nasty to technicians and co-workers. She even cursed the assistant director. She seems terribly nervous and insecure as though she's undergoing some kind of emotional upheaval. Miller stands in the wings, watching her like a faithful hounddog, with a sad lost look in his eyes. Could their marriage be on the rocks?"

My brother had put his finger on the truth. But this was not the only reason Marilyn was upset during the filming. In September, while on location at the Hotel Del Coronado, a seaside resort near San Diego, she wrote me a sad and lonely letter.

She told me she was pregnant again—about four or five weeks, she thought. Her feelings were terribly torn—she should be happy, but she wasn't. She was depressed and, she admitted, scared. The pain was growing worse and her breasts were intensely sore. She wanted the child she had struggled so hard for, but now she didn't. Not really—not deep down. What was she to do? Her and Arthur's marriage, she wrote, was like a sinking ship, and she had no one to cling to, no life preserver. She said Arthur was cold and remote, that he really didn't want the baby; maybe that was why she had been such a meanie lately. She admitted that she was taking out all her anger and frustration on everybody else. In a flash of sympathy, she wrote that poor Arthur looked terribly tired—no doubt from holding her together—and she thought that inside he was as confused and unhappy as she was. He used to try to be pleasant—to pretend everything was okay. But now he sulked, silent and withdrawn inside his shell.

During the third month of her pregnancy, in November 1958, Marilyn lost her second baby by miscarriage. This loss was harder to bear than the first, and it left her in a severe depression all through the winter. While Miller worked on the final draft of *The Misfits,* she consumed large quantities of alcohol and barbituates to reduce her feeling of emptiness and inadequacy. As she considered every failed relationship a betrayal, now she felt nature had betrayed her.

But again her great resiliency came to her aid. When *Some Like It Hot* opened to rave reviews in March, Marilyn looked lovely in a sequined gown at the première, a sober, enigmatic Miller at her side. Soon after, her ego got another boost when she received the David di Donatello award of the Italian Cultural Institute for her performance in *The Prince and the Showgirl,* the only acting award of any significance that she would ever receive. Though it was not an Academy Award, it did reflect the highest recognition of merit by the European film community. It bolstered her spirits sufficiently to give her the courage in June to enter Lenox Hill Hospital in New York for corrective surgery she hoped would enable her to have a child. After days of soul-searching, she had decided that as long as she and Miller were together it would be worth another try. Too involved in *The Misfits* really to care, he acquiesced, hoping it would decrease her inner turmoil and make her less demanding of his attention. He was tired of being the central pillar of her life.

For her birthday earlier that June, I had sent her one of my favorite books. She replied in a short note that it had been a lovely surprise to find *The Little Prince* on her doorstep. She said she loved the line, "The eyes are blind. One must think with the heart"; that said it all, she felt. She thanked me with a kiss for remembering her birthday (a lipstick kiss was imprinted in the margin), and sent a big thank you for all the books, for the notes that accompanied them. She cherished them all, she said. And me.

*"When I'm late or don't show up, it costs the studio thousands of dollars. ...How else can I get a fair deal? I'm not unionized, you know."*

I n Marilyn's last two films, *Let's Make Love* and *The Misfits*, what went on behind the scenes was far more fascinating than the films themselves. In fact, the script of Marilyn's own life was the finest role she ever played. I told her this once and she laughed. "Hey, no wonder my movies are so dull," she said. But she never was.

In February 1960 the cameras should have been stationed in the plush bungalows of the Beverly Hills Hotel where the Millers were residing, and where their neighbors were Marilyn's leading man, Yves Montand, and his actress wife, Simone Signoret.

Miller had known the Montands since they had starred in the French production of his play *The Crucible*. It was no accident that Miller recommended that the French actor, who was then relatively unknown and could hardly speak English, be signed to co-star with Marilyn. That he was good comedian and song and dance man helped. "Anyone who could make her smile came as a blessing to me," Miller was heard to say. His marriage to Marilyn had turned him into a round-the-clock guardian of an emotional cripple who drained both his creative talent and personal identity. He could

129

no longer bear the demeaning errands, the rudeness she subjected him to in public. He hated the routine of filmmaking and the phoniness of Hollywood. He had to have relief. He needed privacy and time for his work. He knew that Montand's Gallic charm could provide breathing space—Montand even looked like a French version of DiMaggio. Perhaps, too, this was a means whereby Miller, when the time came, could slowly disengage himself from marital misery without feeling guilt.

Before *Let's Make Love* got under way, the Millers and the Montands were a congenial foursome, sharing spaghetti dinners and drinking Chianti and spending many enjoyable evenings together. The men played gin rummy, the women chatted. Marilyn admired Simone's sophistication, her confidence, and her stoic acceptance of life, as well as her competence as an actress. They often went shopping together and lazed beside the hotel swimming pool. To Simone, Marilyn seemed charming in her naive, direct way, without any big-star pretensions.

"Yves and Simone are such a delight," Marilyn told me on the phone in March, soon after shooting started. "I'm not depressed anymore, or pill-popping or drinking as much. Yves and I go to work every morning in the studio limousine. We come together about five. He has a wonderful sense of humor, and he seems so confident and calm compared to me. Whenever I drink too much coffee, he scolds me in a sweet, fatherly fashion, 'Ma chérie, that makes you all the more nervous.' Now I don't need cups of black coffee. He's so kind and thoughtful that I've lost a lot of my nervousness."

Marilyn herself was being very kind and thoughtful to everybody on the set, perhaps to impress Montand with her spirit of cooperation. More likely it was to impress Miller, when he visited, with the soothing effect Montand was having on her nerves.

Nonetheless, *Let's Make Love* was a dull movie, perhaps her dullest. The only notable scene was a musical number, "My Heart Belongs to Daddy," which had required eleven days of her sweat and toil to produce this amazing six-minute sequence on film, performed with such apparent naturalness and spontaneity. "But nothing came easily to Marilyn," Maurice Zolotow has observed, "not her beauty, not her personality, not her acting. Facing the gaping camera eye still did not come easily."

Neither Marilyn nor Montand seemed to care about the dullness of *Let's Make Love*. They were too wrapped up in each other. They were seen alone together more and more often, on and off the set. Montand was on his first visit to Hollywood and Marilyn joyfully showed him the sights. The pair

*With George Cukor and Yves Montand at her thirty-second birthday
celebration on the set of* Let's Make Love, *1960.*

made no effort to be secretive; on the contrary, they posed for photographers, flaunting their romance. Their obvious affair struck the film capital like a bombshell, and the shock waves were felt everywhere. Gossip columnists fanned the flames. Why had Miller gone to New York, leaving them to their own devices? Was Simone Signoret's departure for Rome really necessary? Had they both chucked their mates?

During this maelstrom of gossip, I arrived in Los Angeles in early June and phoned Marilyn to say hello. I thought she'd be far too busy to see me, but I was mistaken.

"Where are you staying?" She sounded happy to hear my voice.

"The Beverly Wilshire."

"Oh, great!" she exclaimed. "That's not far. I'll be right over—hey, you do want to see me?"

"Gosh, yes," I stammered.

Marilyn arrived at my door an hour later in a cloud of Chanel No. 5, her blue eyes sparkling, an ebullient smile on her face. She wore black silk slacks, white blouse, sandals, no makeup, and a scarf over her hair. "Oh, Shutterbug," she greeted me with a hug and a kiss, "it's so good to see you."

We sat down on the couch and I poured Dom Perignon. She sipped her drink, smiling. "My favorite champagne—you remembered."

"Be prepared. That's my motto." Then I asked her about Montand. "I must say," I looked her over, "whatever you're doing agrees with you. You look positively superb. But won't the scandal hurt you?"

She shook her head. "In Hollywood there's no such thing as bad publicity."

I was amazed. Hedda Hopper and nearly all the columnists, not to mention large religious groups, had condemned her behavior with Montand. "Are you sure?"

She looked amused. "Remember the nude calendar? What a furor the studio and press made over it? Well, it gave me publicity just when I needed it most. The moral climate of Hollywood is changing. Soon there'll be no taboos. Speaking of publicity, I'll let you in on a secret. You know how the studio gets upset when I'm late?"

"Yes."

"Well, sometimes I'm late deliberately. Other times I call in sick when I'm really not."

"Why?" I asked, astounded.

"It's my secret weapon. When I'm late or don't show up, it costs the studio thousands of dollars. They're always treating me like a thing. With no brains or rights. How else can I get a fair deal? I'm not unionized, you know." She giggled. "Besides, I always make the papers when I don't show up. It draws attention to the picture and keeps the public aware of Marilyn Monroe."

I knew Marilyn was a shrewd publicist, but I feared she had gone too far. "Isn't it dangerous? I mean, what if you really were sick? Nobody would believe you."

She began to laugh. "It's not a question of belief, silly. The studio brass has no choice. I'm their bread and butter. Besides, I give them back valuable publicity, far more than my absences cost them. Why do you think I've made such a spectacle of my affair with Montand?"

"Publicity, I suppose."

"Right," Marilyn declared. "*Let's Make Love* needs it badly. Arthur and I agreed on one thing. It's a dud."

Marilyn went on to say that all she did was work when she came to Hollywood, and now for once she was having lots of fun, going to swanky restaurants and night spots with Yves.

"Where's Arthur now?" I asked.

"In Nevada, looking over locations for *The Misfits*."

"He just walked out?"

Marilyn nodded somberly. "He knows how much I need him when I work. I think he did it to hurt me."

"Maybe he's trying to tell you something."

"No, he's getting back at me, turning on the screws."

I didn't understand. "Why?"

Her eyes were sad. "I'll tell you someday. It's a long story. Right now I don't want to think about it. I want to have fun. Enjoy life. Something old Grumpy Grumps doesn't understand."

Marilyn was silent. Her finger gently traced the rim of her glass. When she started to speak again, she could have been talking to herself. "It started out so beautifully. I was terribly in love. I wanted children, a happy home, a loving husband. It all seemed so simple and possible, like a birthright given to everyone. Now . . . well, it's all gone. There's nothing left between us." She looked up at me, her eyes brimming with tears. "Oh, God—if we could only break up. Call it quits. But we can't. There's still *The Misfits* to do. We're both so heavily committed we can't back out." She drew in her breath. "Meanwhile, I've been terribly lonely. I had to have somebody—something to hold on to. Yves is very understanding. He's so sweet and kind." She tried to smile.

I reached over and put my hand on hers. "Do you love him?" Marilyn was not promiscuous. She never stepped out on a man unless the affair was over.

"Yes. Very much."

My face must have shown a tinge of doubt. She said quickly, "You don't believe me, do you? You think I'm on the rebound. Well, it's not true. I genuinely love Yves."

She was looking for support, but I had to be honest—I cared for her too much. "Listen, isn't it awfully soon? I mean, you hardly know him."

"I can't help it if I fall in love easily. Besides, we're not strangers. We've been living and working closely together for weeks. Yves won't let me down."

"He can't afford to," I pointed out. "Not now, at least. He needs your good will to keep his job. After all, you're giving a little known actor a very lucky break. He has no choice other than to go along with you. Play it casual. Then you won't get hurt."

"I can't treat love casually," she cried. "If I don't commit myself—put my heart and soul into it—I might live to regret it. Besides, what have I got to lose?"

"Your pride," I said. "You don't always want to be a loser, certainly not a laughingstock. You've been through enough pain. A smoldering marriage is the worst kind of hell. Especially when you're bonded together by necessity."

"Yes, I know."

I reminded Marilyn of what she had told me in a letter, that the Montands were deeply devoted to each other, "as ideally married as two people can get." Then for good measure I mentioned that Europeans had the habit of not taking their extramarital affairs too seriously.

She looked at me as if she had not heard a word. "He loves me. That's all that counts."

"Did he say so?"

She shook her head slowly. "I just know."

There was a short silence. Marilyn's eyes met mine and she said wistfully, "Wish the best for me."

I promised I would.

Shortly after that conversation, there's a note in my journal:

> At lunch I said to Austin, chalk one up for French chivalry. Montand is not stringing Marilyn along any more than he can help. He's too attached to Simone. I don't think he believed me.

During the peak of the Marilyn-Montand gossip, Miller grew worried that the affair might become something more than a dalliance and throw a monkey wrench into the filming of *The Misfits*. He dispatched Norman Rosten, who was in Paris, to call on Simone. She had heard about the rumored romance but dismissed it lightly. A devoted Gallic spouse, she was willing to turn her head. Her only concern was for the safety of their marriage and the possible effect the episode might have on her husband's career.

Marilyn went to New York's Idlewild Airport, unannounced, to meet Montand on his way back to Paris. They shared a bottle of Dom Perignon in the back of a limousine. It was a sad moment for Marilyn. "He tried to be tender and sweet," she sobbed when she told me about it. "And he kissed my cheek and all that. But he said that he couldn't possibly leave Simone and that we should forget each other."

Later, with Montand safely at her side, Simone Signoret told reporters, "A man doesn't feel he has to confuse an affair with eternal love and make it a crisis in marriage."

But the marriage of Marilyn and Miller was entering its final round, with both partners like two punched-out boxers, praying for the bell. It would toll slowly and painfully in the scorching desert heat of Nevada during Marilyn's last completed film, the memorable *Misfits*.

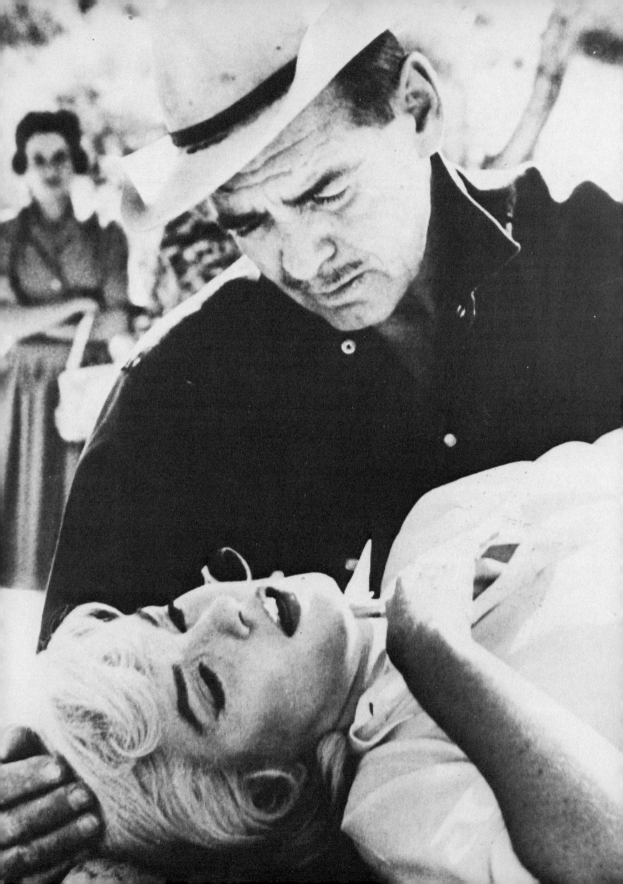

*"You're not worried about me. All
you're worried about is that nothing
fouls up your goddamned movie."*

*I*n July 1960 the production company of *The Misfits* assembled
in Reno. But Marilyn was in no condition physically or emotionally to start another picture so soon. She was exhausted from filming
*Let's Make Love* and despondent over her rejection by Montand. The inevitable question arose to plague her. Why was happiness denied her? The
love goddess of the world was starved for love. The irony festered deep in
her, creating an eternity of sleepless nights and her severest depressions.
But the more life became too much for Marilyn, the more the public seemed
to adore her.

Together now in name only, the Millers had taken a suite on the top floor
of the Mapes Hotel, in which would be acted out the final scene of their ill-
fated marriage. In public Miller assumed the role of distant relative, polite
but remote. He and Marilyn were seldom seen together. In his place at her
side now was Paula Strasberg, in her customary black, hovering about Marilyn
like an overly attentive mother hen.

When shooting began, during the day Marilyn was the shy, vulnerable
Roslyn Taber; each night she was the wife of the playwright she had grown

137

*With Clark Gable during the filming of* The Misfits, *1960.*

to despise and whom she would not forgive for passing her off on another man.

Heralded as "the ultimate motion picture," *The Misfits* was directed by John Huston; its cast included Clark Gable, Montgomery Clift, Eli Wallach, and Thelma Ritter. Marilyn worshiped Gable. They had met years earlier at a Hollywood party, and as they danced that evening she had told him that he was the father she had always wished she had. Gable was flattered and loved her frankness. A man of considerable compassion, he took a paternal interest in Marilyn all through the film.

Shooting began with hoopla and fanfare and good intentions, but soon became an endurance test for everyone involved. Time after time Marilyn was late or too ill to show up. When she did appear, she came to the set groggy from sleeping pills. If Huston was angry, he didn't show it. He maintained a professional attitude of cordiality, while Miller stood nervously between director and star.

But it soon became obvious to Huston, and to everyone else, that Marilyn was terribly ill, either emotionally or physically, and that Miller was unable to do anything about it. Some even blamed her condition on him, but in fact Miller was close to exhaustion himself from caring for his wife. He could not risk leaving Marilyn alone in her precarious emotional state. He nursed her through the long nights, rationing the pills she consumed so that she wouldn't take too many. The constant vigil sapped his strength. He grew haggard and neglected his work, the constant rewriting of the script. They spoke to each other less and less. Marilyn would ignore him or lash out: "Christ, leave me alone. You're not worried about me. All you're worried about is that nothing fouls up your goddamned movie." Still, Miller continued to watch over her. "She needs care at night," he was heard to say, as though he willingly accepted the suffering as absolution for his past behavior.

After almost six weeks of shooting, Marilyn collapsed. Huston shut down the set and had her flown to Los Angeles. Suffering from acute nervous exhaustion, she was admitted to Westside Hospital. I was in Los Angeles myself at the time, visiting my mother, who had suffered a stroke.

Austin said Westside Hospital security was so tight I wouldn't be able to get in to see M. But I did—as Dr. Revonoc. Marilyn looked pale and weary, but was delighted to see me. I asked her what happened? What was she doing here? She said she couldn't stand Arthur anymore. She had to get away from him. All he thinks about is his damn career—his damn movie. I said—didn't he write it for you? That's what he told me.

*En route to Nevada to film* The Misfits, *July 1960.*

It was to be *our* movie. But he lied, he lied. All he wanted was to use me to regain his prestige. I'll never forgive him, never. She began to cry. It's terrible. I can't trust anybody anymore, not anybody. I tried to comfort her, but she went on: Roslyn was supposed to be me. But she isn't—she's too wishywashy. Arthur changed the script. She's not like me at all. All he cares about are the men. They are everything, I am merely a drawing card to get people into the theatres. I couldn't understand. Why did Arthur change the script? Because he's a creep— he kowtows to Huston and lets him constantly rewrite the lines. Now Roslyn has no depth—just this hang-up on horses. She's almost an incident to the story. But, I said, the director has the final authority, doesn't he? She said, maybe so. But Arthur should stand up to Huston. He's gutless. He's letting Huston ruin the film. I thought it best to let M. talk, so I said nothing. Huston is like a tough kid. Always has to have his own way. I think he's arrogant and rude. Women to him are just brainless creatures to be put up with. He calls me honey just to irritate me. I get so mad sometimes I could kick him in the balls. But what can you expect—he's in Arthur's camp. Oh well, Marilyn shrugged, it'll be all over soon. I've been taking too many Nembutals. But I'm okay now. A few more days rest and I'll be out, the doctor said.

Out but not okay, I thought. Back in Reno she would again have to face the hideous tension of the set, live in daily contact with Miller, and contend with the searing pain of the knowledge that she could not hold on to anyone for long, that in the near future would come the awful process of divorce. Any or all of which could undermine her precarious grip on reality.

I thought it best to change the subject. I asked her, "How did you and Gable hit it off?"

"Oh, great." She beamed. "He's so kind and sweet and patient with me. And so modest, it's unbelievable. He's just like you told me. A perfect gentleman. It's a dream come true, being able to play opposite him. I'll remember and treasure the memory always."

If Marilyn saw in Gable a father figure, she recognized in Montgomery Clift a kindred soul: "He's even got more hang-ups than me." She laughed. "What's more, he can't sleep either. He's so terrified at being unable to sleep he had his bed shipped out from New York. I shouldn't laugh. I really feel sorry for him, Shutterbug. That car accident has left him so frail and sick. He's on drugs and drinks constantly. He needs somebody to look after him."

140

The Misfits: *clockwise, Marilyn, Montgomery Clift, producer Frank Taylor, Eli Wallach, Arthur Miller, John Huston, Clark Gable.*

Monty and Marilyn were on the same wavelength. They were psychic twins, both terribly sensitive, shy and nervous people who recognized their handicaps and were able to laugh at them.

I noticed Marilyn was coughing a great deal, a harsh throaty hack that was definitely unpleasant for her. "That's a wicked cough," I said, getting her a glass of water.

"It's that dry Nevada desert. Everybody has it. Some days the air is so thick with alkali dust you can hardly breathe." She drained the glass, then pointed to the foot of the bed, where a manuscript lay. "Would you like to read *The Misfits?*"

"Sure. I'd love to. I'll take it with me . . . ."

"No. Read it here." She smiled, grasping my arm. "I enjoy your company."

I looked at my watch. "I've been here an hour. You're probably tired and need the rest."

"Hey, don't be so silly." She grinned affectionately at me and handed me the script. "I'm eager to know what you think of it."

While she buried herself in a book, I sat in the metal chair beside her and went through the script carefully. "I see what you mean," I said at last. "It reads like an ode to male virility. You know, 'manliness.' "

"Huston would agree," Marilyn said, "but Arthur would say individualism."

"I don't know how it'll go over. It's almost plotless. All the characters do is yak at each other. As for the ending, I think Roslyn should have gone off with Clift."

"Why?"

"He's young. He represents the future. Gable is much too paternal a figure. It's like a girl running off with her father."

"Funny. That's what Monty said. He thought Arthur identified with Gay Langland [the character Gable played], and couldn't stand anyone getting Roslyn except himself. But I think the public expects Gable to get the girl. They still see him in his prime. Not the nearly sixty-year-old he is. So I agree with Arthur's ending."

Then a nurse came in with medicine for Marilyn, and I slipped out quietly to visit the men's room. When I returned, Marilyn was by the window, standing there in bare feet and black negligée, gazing at the traffic below. "Shutterbug, I'm scared. I can't go back to Reno. I can't . . . I can't." An edge of hysteria was in her voice. "I can't face Arthur again. Go through each day seeing his grouchy face, being treated like a child. Christ! I can't stand his groveling. All he thinks about is that cursed movie. I'm not going back. I'll break up. I know I will." She started to cry, burying her head in her hands.

I took her in my arms, and I just held her and gently stroked her head. "Oh, no, you won't," I said, "because you've got something infinitely more precious than talent. You've got spunk."

Her face was against my chest and I could feel the warm moisture of her tears. Slowly she calmed down and lifted up her face and tried to smile. "You really think so?"

"Yes. You've got more real guts than anybody I know."

"I'm sorry," she said with a forlorn smile. "It just all came out."

I held her shoulders and looked at her. "Listen, Sweetheart. You know what you're going to do? When you return to Reno, you're going to pretend Arthur isn't there. That he really doesn't exist. You're going to prove to yourself that you are a great actress. Not only before the camera, but off camera. So don't fluff it." I kissed her shiny nose. "Okay?"

Her eyes were smiling now, too. "Okay."

I helped her into bed and tucked the covers around her. She looked up at me. "You know something, Shutterbug?"

"No, what?"

She giggled. "You're as good as a shrink."

Austin didn't believe that I saw M. for three hours this afternoon until I told him a detailed account of our conversation. He looked amazed. Tiny, he said, you should've been a reporter. I nearly choked.

When Marilyn returned to Nevada a week later, her enforced vacation had worked wonders. As the film resumed shooting, she was punctual, full of laughter; she talked with everyone except Miller and his closest friend, Eli Wallach. She spent her spare time now with members of her entourage, mostly with Ralph Roberts, her masseur, Whitey Snyder, her makeup man, and Paula Strasberg.

Near the end of filming, Gable said, "If *The Misfits* inspires a younger generation sufficiently to even think about being themselves, it'll help."

The finished film lasted 124 minutes on the screen; unfortunately it didn't last long in the theatres. But all agreed that Marilyn had given one of her finest performances.

*"A career is wonderful, but you
can't curl up with it on a cold night."*

When *The Misfits* was finished in November 1960, Marilyn returned to New York to an empty apartment and announced her
separation from Miller. Confronted with divorce, she was engulfed by a deep
sense of failure, with nothing to look forward to but a bleak future of loneliness.

Then came the news that Clark Gable, "The King," had died of a heart
attack. As I grieved for my friend, I knew Marilyn would be shocked and
deeply distressed. She revered him as if he were her father. His presence,
more than anything else, had given her the courage to finish *The Misfits*.
Later, when Kay Gable put the blame for her husband's untimely death on
Marilyn's shoulders, I knew Marilyn would be devastated. "Listen," I told
her on the phone, "you're not to blame for Gable's death. He had a heart
condition. It's not your fault."

"But I was always late," she sobbed. "I kept him waiting in that hundred-
degree heat. Oh, God, how could I've been so thoughtless. I loved him,
Shutterbug. I really did. And I killed him. Oh, God, forgive me."

Patiently I explained repeatedly that Gable's death had nothing to do with

145

her. Slowly something seemed to relax inside her, and I heard her catch her breath. "Maybe you're right," she said at last. "You always seem to be." Her voice was weary and far away.

"Dr. Revonoc knows best. Now I've got a prescription. Get the hell out of that apartment and have some fun. Call Joe or Frankie. Keep busy and think positive. Okay?"

"Okay," came the breathless voice.

"Now smile," I ordered. "No, wider. That's it. A smile is the only antidote for tears."

I heard a slight sob, then she blurted out, "Oh, Shutterbug, I don't know how to say it—though I hardly ever see you, it's nice to know that somewhere out there, there's someone like you."

A few weeks later, it pleased me greatly to hear that once again she was seeing DiMaggio. He was the one solid rock in her life she could cling to for support and comfort. After her divorce from Miller on January 20, 1961, the day of John Kennedy's inauguration, she would need him more than ever before. She was on the brink of the severest depression of her life.

Her divorce and the cool reception accorded *The Misfits*, and her increasing loneliness, plunged Marilyn into such a state of despair that Dr. Kris, her New York analyst, became alarmed. Marilyn was admitted to the Payne-Whitney Psychiatric Clinic of New York Hospital and found herself in the wing for the mentally ill. She was terrified as iron doors closed behind her. "Where are you taking me?" she demanded. The room was like a cell, with barred windows and a glass pane in the door through which the medical staff could check on her.

Later she told her press secretary, Pat Newcomb, "If they think I'm a nut, I'm going to act like one"; she had raved and torn her hospital gown into shreds.

On the third day, she called DiMaggio for help. Joe came quickly and had her transferred to Columbia Presbyterian Hospital, where she began to recuperate with the help of his presence, flowers, and candy.

After three weeks of rest, Marilyn returned to her 57th Street apartment revitalized and humming with plans. She made preparations to do Somerset Maugham's *Rain* for NBC-TV, and told a reporter, "I like the part of Sadie Thompson. She's a girl who knows how to be gay even when she's sad. And that's important, you know." But the production was canceled at the last moment, and Marilyn flew off to Florida, where the Yankees were in spring training, to be with Joe.

Soon she seemed her old self, carefree and gay; in pictures taken of the

146

*In Florida watching Joe DiMaggio coaching Yankee batting practice,*
*March 1961.*

two together they look still very much in love. Gossip began to snowball that they were headed for the altar. When Austin called to say that it looked like they were going to try it again, I phoned Marilyn to congratulate her.

"For what?" she asked.

"Aren't you and Joe getting hitched again?"

"Oh, no. That's newspaper stuff. Joe and I are just good friends."

She said that marriage to Joe would be the same mistake, that her career was now the most important thing and that she'd soon be going back to Hollywood. "But I'll keep my apartment here. It's fun having two separate lives and two different sets of friends. Geminis need the change."

Marilyn was thirty-five now and still insecure in her emotions, in her health, and in her career. "Don't you think it's time you should put down roots?" I asked. "I mean, buy a house. It would give you a sense of security."

"I can't ever imagine buying a home alone."

"Well, think about it anyway."

"Okay, I'll try."

I told Marilyn how glad I was that she had decided on Hollywood, that she really didn't belong in the theatre.

"Why?" she asked.

"I don't believe you have the stamina, the discipline, or the temperament. You're a unique child of the screen, with a very great talent. You should go on to perfect that talent. And ask yourself honestly: 'Could I make a curtain, night after night?' "

"Hmm . . . probably not," she admitted.

"You've mastered movie techniques," I said. "Why not stick with something you know and do well?"

"But I never get the films I want to do."

"You will. You did before with Greene."

"You really think so?"

"Absolutely."

I reminded her of what Billy Wilder had said in the press about her: "Marilyn doesn't need to go to Actor's Lab. She was born just as good as she'll ever be—and that's damn good!"

"Hey, that's nice," she breathed.

I was pleased that in coming to the Coast Marilyn would be breaking away from the Actors Studio. I shared Wilder's distaste for method acting because I felt that in many respects it had done Marilyn far more harm than good. It had failed to give her talent the underlay of confidence she so desperately

148

needed and wasted much of her working time on "preparation." Far too much emphasis was put on the performer's feelings and not enough value placed on discipline; this imbalance made her entirely dependent on coaches like Paula Strasberg for support and seemed only to increase her insecurities.

I suspected that Lee Strasberg's relationship with Marilyn might be a little more than one of teacher to pupil, although I had little to substantiate my feeling other than the tenacious, almost hypnotic, hold he had on Marilyn and the fact that she idolized him as if he were a saint. Since his teaching methods brought her personal problems to light, he also became her confessor and analyst, and teacher and pupil were drawn ever more closely together. But at least he filled in the gap of loneliness left by Miller.

On numerous occasions Marilyn spoke of her loneliness to Frank Sinatra, whom she had been seeing when he visited New York, and she told him that what she really missed was the basset hound, Hugo, she had left in the country with Miller. Frank's gift to her of a little white poodle (she named him Maf) meant more to her than any ermine stole or diamond necklace. It was the nicest gift Marilyn had ever received. Maf proved just the company she needed to help her get through this difficult time.

Frank was a friend whom Marilyn could trust and depend on for good counsel. Also, his companionship was a tonic that never failed to perk up her spirits. "After one night with Frankie," Marilyn told me, "I don't have to see my analyst for weeks."

When Marilyn moved back to California she stayed in Frank's new Beverly Hills house until she found a place of her own. He was in Italy at the time, making a film, and he kidded his companions, "I date a lot of gals, but I've got Marilyn living in my bedroom."

A few months later, not long after she moved into her Doheny Drive apartment, she wrote to me: "I'm so excited. I think Frankie is going to marry me. He said last night, 'I think we'd make a good team. We're both in show biz, have careers, like to laugh and have lots of fun.' Gee, he's sweet. Always so kind and thoughtful. And a real gentleman. I love him dearly. I'll have no sleepless nights with him. Oh, Shutterbug, please wish the best for me."

I was worried. Sinatra was too much of a ladies' man and far too wrapped up in himself. A man of shortlived enthusiasms, his own restless nature was hardly the climate to make Marilyn feel secure and happy in the close atmosphere of marriage. So it came as a relief and no surprise the following month to hear he had been stepping out with Juliet Prowse and was planning to marry her, but I felt sorry for Marilyn. Her life seemed to be one rejection after another. No woman ever needed more a reliable and supportive husband.

Marilyn needed someone who not only loved her but who understood her and accepted her and made her feel secure. But all she had, even when she was married to them, was a series of lovers. No one had given her total commitment; perhaps nobody could. I was glad that Joe stood in the wings, available whenever she needed him.

I had serious reservations about Marilyn's capacity to live alone, just as I had about her capacity to choose that right man to marry. As always, she made no bones about her faults. "I don't know why," she admitted, "but the men I find I'm most attracted to are those least capable of making me happy." The statement was true, of course, and sad.

Everything seemed to be so difficult for Marilyn, even sleep. Nothing came easy for her except falling in love, and there was something sad about that and in her words, "I'm only happy when I'm in love."

Her openness and vulnerability were the cornerstones of Marilyn's charm, but they also brought her the most trouble and pain. Soon, I knew, she would be head over heels in love again. This time, I hoped, it would be with someone solid and worthy. I wanted her to know happiness before it was too late.

*"He's a wonderful writer, you know.*
*A much better writer than a husband.*
*He's too much of an introvert to be a*
*good companion. I would have been*
*happier with a man who knew how to*
*laugh and play."*

Marilyn and I met again in December 1961, when we were both in California. She was still living in her Doheny Drive apartment, not far from Sunset Strip.

She is more lovely than ever, and very pleased to see me. The apartment I found unattractive and sterile looking, without character or warmth. At the first opportunity I asked her if she wouldn't be happier if she had her own home. She said that's what her psychiatrist said—a Dr. Greenson—and went on to tell me how much she liked him. Frankie, she said, told me about him. I didn't like shrinks, but I said that he's right about the house. That it would give her a sense of security. When she told me how often she saw him I did become suspicious and asked if he was in real estate too. I felt badly after I said that. I have to talk to someone, she replied.

Marilyn seemed in good spirits and looked really great. She wore no makeup, yet her face glowed from her obvious well-being; her eyes were

*With Arthur Miller at a screening of* Some Like It Hot, *February 5, 1960.*

clear and cool and as blue as mountain skies. Perhaps this doctor had been good for her, but I hated to see her get hooked to the point where she couldn't function without him. That could mean trouble, I told her, and it worried me.

"That's sweet." She smiled at me.

"Well, I'm concerned."

"Thanks." She kissed my check. "You needn't worry. I feel better than I have in a long time. And I know he's largely responsible."

"And what if this chap takes off on a holiday where he can't be reached?" She thought for a moment. "I'd be in a bad way, I guess."

"Would you like a suggestion?"

"Sure."

I looked into her eyes. "Ease off a little, Sweetheart. It's for your own good."

Marilyn said she would try, but I felt she had become far too dependent on him to make any serious attempt. An uncomfortable silence settled between us. I thought at this point a little humor might be timely. "Just for kicks," I said to Marilyn, "stretch out on the couch and tell Dr. Revonoc your problems." I grinned at her. "There's no charge."

"Okay." She stretched out, displaying her legs and providing an attractive glimpse of her breasts as her blue polka dot robe fell away from her shoulders. I said, "Now tell me your main problem, madame?"

"Sex." She giggled.

"Too little or too much?"

"Oh, much too little."

I was becoming self-conscious. "Ah, hmm. I'm afraid I can't . . ."

"Oh, but you can." She pulled me to the couch, giggling, and began to shower my face with kisses. I suddenly felt as if I were in a scene from one of Marilyn's comedies. I extricated myself from her arms and took up a more dignified position at her side. "I think, maybe," I stammered, "we should keep this therapy purely on a professional basis."

"Oh, Shutterbug, you're so funny. Don't you have any animal instinct?"

"Yes, I mean, no." I tried to straighten my tie. "I mean . . . I really don't know what I mean."

She broke into laughter, "I can see that." Then her mood changed, as it often did, swiftly and with no apparent reason. She suddenly looked very lonely and small and forlorn. "Is there something wrong with me?" she cried. "Nobody loves me anymore."

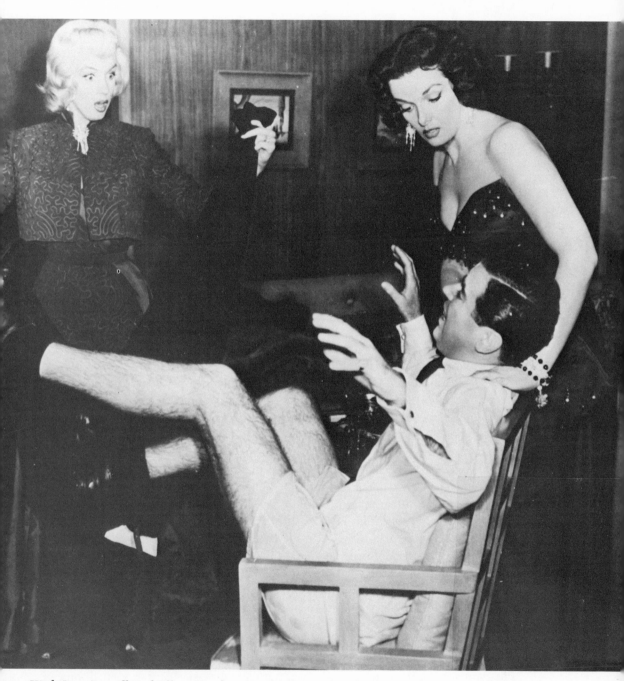

*With Jane Russell and Elliott Reed in* Gentlemen Prefer Blondes, *1953.*

I put my arms around her and tried to comfort her. She seemed a totally different person, and I didn't know what to say. "Listen," I began uncertainly, "millions of people love you. You're the most adored woman in the world."

"Yeah, but no man loves me," she sobbed. "All they want is a plaything."

I looked into her tear-streaked face. "I'm sure Joe loves you. And Sinatra. And Whitey Snyder."

"How about you? Do you love me?"

"Yes. Very much."

"Enough to marry me?"

The question took me off guard, and I felt confused and embarrassed. "Yes," I said finally. "If I thought it would work. You know love and marriage aren't always compatible. In our case, it would be a terrible mistake."

"Why?" She studied me closely. "What makes you so sure?"

"Our lifestyles. They're poles apart. Worse than yours and DiMaggio's. Or yours and Miller's. You wouldn't be happy living on an island. I wouldn't be happy living anywhere else. What you need are close friends, trustworthy confidantes. They're much harder to find than husbands."

She laughed, but without humor. "Same old Shutterbug. You Cancers can wiggle out of anything."

"Isn't what I said the truth?"

Her face softened. "Of course. I'm sorry, Shutterbug. I wasn't being fair. I was only feeling sorry for myself." Her eyes still shone with tears, but she was trying to smile. "It's just that I'm in a foul mood. Forgive me."

"Everybody gets that way at times." I patted her hand sympathetically.

"You don't."

"Oh, yes, I do," I said, smiling. "It's just that I don't show it. I keep everything bottled up inside. One day I'll explode like a pressure cooker, and you'll have to clean up the mess."

She laughed. "I wish you never had to go. You're such a good sport. You always make me feel better." She sat back, relaxing. "You know, I think you're right. I do need more friends like you, friends who want nothing from me and whom I can trust. It seems like all my friends are people I employ or pay. They all want something from me. I never know whether they're telling the truth—or just trying to please me. It makes me feel frustrated and insecure. Except with the Strasbergs. They've been like father and mother to me. I know they'd never use me or let me down."

"How do you know? You give them money all the time," I reminded her. "Plus you pay Paula nearly two thousand dollars a week salary as your drama coach, which is extremely generous. Besides, they've got a lot to gain by having such a famous student."

"They really need the money, honestly. The studio depends on donations."

I decided to drop this ticklish subject and ask her a question that had long been in my mind. "What happened between you and Arthur? Can you talk about it now?"

She nodded, her eyes somber and reflective. "It's a long story. I think all the trouble really began in England when he found I was difficult to live with when I worked, that I wasn't the sweet, docile little creature that he thought he'd married. Then, one day on Long Island, I asked him why he hadn't written anything in such a long time."

"What did he say?"

"That his previous marriage had sapped his creative energy. He just couldn't write with his whole world collapsing. This sounded very logical. Then, I don't know why, I asked him if this was the only reason. Well, you should have seen his face. It was like I had asked him to shoot himself. 'For Christ's sake,' he bellowed, 'what other reason could there be?' I didn't know what to say, but his reaction told me something I didn't want to believe. He shouted, 'Why don't you say what you were really thinking? That I've dried up—come to a dead end. Finished as a playwright.' I told him I wasn't thinking that, honestly. I just didn't know how to calm him down. He was glaring at me. It was terrible. He grabbed my arm and twisted it, and it hurt, and I wanted to cry. I broke away from him and ran into my room and threw myself on the bed and cried until I had no more tears. Our marriage went downhill from that day. And then, money. Money was never very important to me, but to Arthur it was an obsession. He would never give a tip or pick up a lunch tab. This humiliated me many times. If he had to spend a dime I could see him cringe. Since he was living off my money and I was doing all the work, I found myself losing respect for him. I made up my mind he had to do something for me. If our relationship was to continue, he would have to work for me. And then for the last two and a half years, I made him do just that. And he did, grumbling, of course, at every opportunity. That's when I began calling him Grumpy Grumps. I treated him badly, I know. But he also put me through hell with his explosive temper and endless recriminations. It's never all one way. What hurt him worst was when his friends saw that he became a lackey. I regret this very much. I wasn't out to punish Arthur, just to make him pull his own weight."

"Do you think he can still write?"

*With Arthur Miller, November 1959.*

"Oh, yes. As soon as he sorts himself out. He's a wonderful writer, you know. A much better writer than a husband. He's too much of an introvert to be a good companion. I would have been happier with a man who knew how to laugh and play. It's sad, really. Arthur didn't know how to do either." She smiled. "I've talked enough about myself. What about your book? Have you found a publisher yet?"

"Nope. The manuscript aways comes back. I don't know what's wrong with it."

"I'd like to see it," Marilyn said. I wished I had brought it along. Perhaps she could help—after two years of rejections, I was about ready to give up.

I heard somebody come into the kitchen and the sound of groceries being unloaded from a paper bag. "Who's that?" I asked.

"Oh, that's my new housekeeper, Mrs. Murray. She comes three or four days a week. Dr. Greenson recommended her."

Through the doorway I could see a small, rather sober-looking middle-aged woman putting canned goods into a cupboard. She didn't look like a servant. Her appearance and bearing were that of a very strong woman.

My journal entry about that meeting ends here. I don't remember what happened after that except that Marilyn wanted to see me the next day. But I declined the offer by telling her I had an engagement. I knew my resistance would weaken if I saw her again so soon.

*12305 Fifth Helena Drive, Brentwood, the house that Marilyn bought.*

*"I thought I could never buy a home
alone, but I've done it. It's like being
married and not having a husband."*

In late January 1962, Marilyn, accompanied by her housekeeper-companion, Mrs. Murray, began looking for a house to buy, first along the ocean and then in the vicinity of Westwood. Their search was successful, and in March Marilyn the homeowner wrote to me excitedly.

Breezy and confident in tone, her letter announced that she'd bought a Mexican-style home in Brentwood. She described it to me in loving detail: it was quiet and secluded, at the end of a cul de sac. It had a red tiled roof, thick white walls, sunken windows with wrought iron grilles. Shaded by many trees and flowering vines, it hugged the earth as if it had always been there. At the back, there was an oval swimming pool, a guest house, and lots of bamboo and trees. The rooms had dark, beamed ceilings, the floors were carpeted with white wool; there was very little furniture.

Marilyn was full of plans. Most of the rooms would have to be changed, she wrote. She wanted the house to have a genuine Mexican motif, especially the kitchen, which needed bright tiles and more color. She said she'd like to go to Mexico to buy the furnishings. Proudly, she confided that she'd thought she could never buy a home alone, but she'd done it. It was like being married and not having a husband.

The following month, I was in New York.

Saw three publishers today. Always the same answers. We like your manuscript, but there's no room on our present list. Discouraged, I went up to my hotel room and sat on the bed, thinking I might as well go home. Then I thought I'd give Marilyn's apartment a ring on the off chance she'd be there.

"Hi, where are you?" came the familiar greeting. I told her I was at the Barbizon Plaza and suggested that we meet in the lounge.

"I'll be there at four-thirty," she said.

I'd just finished my second Scotch and soda when Marilyn came into the lounge and walked toward me. She was wearing a blue scarf, a baggy sweater, and little makeup. Her body had lost the bounce and trimness of youth. Her face seemed thinner, paler and more delicate than the last time I'd seen her, and there was a certain sadness in her eyes. It was more a look of loneliness, I decided, as she greeted me with a hug and a kiss on the cheek.

When our drinks came, we touched glasses. "Cheers," she said, beaming as though she hadn't seen a friend in ages. "Did your wife come with you?"

"No. Someone has to hold down the island."

"You mean she's there all alone?"

"Oh, no." I grinned. "My mother-in-law is there. I thought it was a good time to leave."

Marilyn giggled. "What brings you to New York?"

"To flog my book," I told her, pointing to the bulky manuscript next to me.

"Any luck?"

"Nope," I said dejectedly. "I can't figure it out. I thought real-life adventure stories were always in demand, but no publisher will touch it."

"Let me read it."

"Okay. I'd appreciate it." With her ability to evaluate story material, perhaps Marilyn could find the problem.

"When are you going to write about me?" she asked, always concerned with how she could market her image.

"I have." I grinned at her. "In my journals."

"No, I mean for publication."

"Someday, perhaps."

She looked at me. "You can write about me now. I won't mind. I know you'll tell the truth."

"It's not that easy," I said. "You're a very complex subject. Your personality has as many hues as a rainbow."

Marilyn laughed. "You mean, I'm complicated?"

I was a little embarrassed. "But in a nice way. I think I know Norma Jean. But I'm not really sure I know Marilyn Monroe. Because you shift roles constantly, it's difficult to interpret your real feelings. It's as though you can't decide sometimes who you want to be."

She sat back. "That's my problem—I'm torn. Sometimes I don't know who I am. It's like hearing voices, each telling you differently what to say and do. Even how to feel. It's terribly frustrating."

"Maybe that's what makes you so changeable. The reason some people find you difficult to understand."

"I suppose so," she said finally. "And sometimes I find I have more than two sides. I am so many different persons. I definitely change, with places as well as with people. I'm a different person here than I am in Hollywood. I'm different with Whitey Snyder than I am with you. And I'm different again with Lee Strasberg. In fact, I feel that I'm always in a state of change."

"Spoken like a true Gemini. Now will the real Marilyn please stand up." That amused her. She laughed so loudly that people began to stare at us, and I hoped no one would recognize her. She was relaxed now, smiling happily and having fun, and I didn't want anything to spoil the occasion.

"It's funny." Marilyn giggled. "I've got so many selves I wish I knew which one was me. It was confusing at first until I found that some of my friends were that way too. Frankie carries around with him a dozen different people. You're the only person I know who is always the same."

"I must bore you."

"No, on the contrary. I find stable men the most attractive. You know where you stand with them. Their self-confidence—because I have so little— also makes me feel more secure. I thought Arthur was like that at first, but he's as many people as Frankie. None of whom are very nice to live with." Marilyn stopped abruptly, as if she didn't want to go on with the subject, and asked then, "Did you read about the airplane crash? Those eighty people dying needlessly?" I could see her shiver slightly. "It makes me even more conscious of dying. Do you worry about death? I mean, does it bother you sometimes?"

"No. Not really."

"Why?"

"I don't know. I can't worry about something I have no control over."

"I'm afraid of death. But not as much as I am of old age. You should see my arms." She pulled up her sleeve. "Look at these liver spots. They're so ugly. Is this part of aging?"

"Not always." I showed her my own arms. "I've had these ever since I was sixteen."

"Oh, good." Marilyn beamed. "I feel better now."

I'd heard rumors, and I had to ask her. "Have you ever attempted suicide?"

Marilyn shook her head. "Not deliberately. Once or twice I've taken an overdose of sleeping pills. But only accidentally. With Nembutals, you never know when you've had one too many."

"Have you ever thought about suicide?"

"Oh, yes. I believe everyone has at one time or another. I certainly did after Gable's death. I felt so depressed I wanted to jump from my apartment window. But I didn't, of course." She smiled. "No, I don't think I could take my own life. Could you?"

"No."

"You wouldn't really get to know your whole self. I'm much too eager to see how I turn out."

I smiled at her. "So far you've done a marvelous job, Sweetheart. People know the hardships you went through to become famous. You made sure of that. They respect your dedication and courage. But what they most admire is that in becoming Marilyn, you haven't lost the sweetness of Norma Jean."

"I can't seem to shake her." She laughed. "Even if I wanted to. She's my alter ego—very sensitive and easily hurt. Every time someone takes advantage of Norma Jean, I become a real bitch." Her eyes looked into mine. "You've never seen my bitchy side, have you?"

I shook my head. "No. Not really."

The waiter brought another round of drinks. Marilyn took a swallow of hers and said, "Well, I can be a real stinker. When I'm finished with someone—like Natasha—I just bring down the curtain. Bang! That's it! No goodbyes. No I'm sorrys. When I feel betrayed or feel that somebody is patronizing me, bang goes the curtain. I'm a stinker. I've made more enemies than friends, because I trust people too much. I go on trusting them and believing in them long after I shouldn't, and then I get hurt, and that brings out the bitch in me. No one seems honest or sincere anymore. They all want chunks out of me. For a while I tried to please everyone and make everybody around me happy. I gave and gave until I found myself emptied, with nothing

left of my private self that was truly me."

"You're saying that you can't be sweet and survive?"

She nodded emphatically. "But you can't be too thick skinned, either. That kills sensitivity. Besides, you've got to be open to grow. Which means you can get hurt easily."

I asked her how she was making out living alone. "Not very well," she said. "I'm not sure whether I can handle it. But the house helps. It takes up much of my spare time. The worst problem is at night. That's when I hate being alone. Maybe I should get married again. What makes the day really worthwhile is having someone to curl up with at night."

She looked so sad I felt sorry I had brought up the subject. "It would be easier," she went on, "if I could sleep. With no one to talk to, or to take my mind off myself, I have to take a lot more sleeping pills. They do help, but not as much as having a man around. It's frustrating living alone. You turn inward and become more self-centered, and that's not good. You eat poorly, and that's not good either. Then you go out with guys—because you're lonely—you wouldn't look at twice any other time. I know. I've been with some real creeps." She paused. "Hey, do you think masturbation is harmful?"

"Heavens, no," I replied. "It's a natural way to let off pressure."

She looked relieved. But I saw her eyes were slightly glazed, and I was getting a little dizzy. We were both very sloshed.

She leaned towards me and asked, "Do you, I mean—do you—"

"Yes," I admitted.

She looked mischievous. "Hey, maybe we should get together. It would solve both our problems."

I laughed. "So we're back to that subject."

"I'm still not sold on your argument that we shouldn't." I thought it best not to order another round of drinks.

"I suspected as much."

"I consider it quite a rejection, you know."

I reached over and touched her hand. "I didn't mean it that way. Without a doubt you are the most desirable woman in the world. Most men would kick me in the ass."

"Most women, too." She giggled.

At least, I thought, she was treating the subject lightly. But as often happened, her mood changed swiftly, and she suddenly became very serious. "Believe me, I don't try to seduce every man I meet. I only like having sex with men I care about. It's more meaningful, not just an animal thing. You

166

really try to satisfy the other person. Besides, it's the nicest way I know to get to sleep. Don't you think so?"

I agreed, with some reluctance.

"Come on," she said gleefully, jumping to her feet. "Let's go to my apartment and enjoy ourselves."

"Wait," I said. "Sit down. I haven't finished my drink."

"I've got plenty of Dom Perignon chilled."

"I have an appointment with a publisher," I lied awkwardly. "Let me have a raincheck."

"We could go up to your room." She look so sad and dejected standing there, I felt like a perfect heel.

"I'm afraid there isn't time." I patted the seat. "Please sit down."

With an exasperated sigh, she sat. "Don't you love me?"

"Of course I do, Sweetheart. Very much." I squeezed her hand. "Look into my eyes. There." Her eyes were full on mine. "Am I not telling you the truth?"

She nodded feebly. "I don't understand. Why don't you show me that you love me?"

"Don't I?"

"No, you won't go to bed with me. What's the matter? Doesn't sex interest you anymore?"

I assured her that it did. "I just think a man and a woman can be good friends without it."

Marilyn was silent for a moment. "You're afraid to let yourself go, aren't you?"

I thought about that. "Yes, frankly," I admitted.

"For one night?" She stared at me. "Why?"

I could feel my face redden. I was embarrassed to tell her the truth, yet I knew there was no other choice. Finally the words came. "Because if I did, I'd never want to leave you."

She put her hand on mine. "Hey, that's sweet, Shutterbug. I think you really do love me." There were tears in her eyes as she gazed at me fondly. "You know what I wish?" She smiled.

"No."

"That I was still Norma Jean. The simple girl you first met. And that she loved to cook and keep house and loved the outdoors."

"I wish that too."

"Odd, isn't it? We both have everything we want, except . . ."

"Happiness?"

"Yes."

"Don't worry, Sweetheart." I forced a smile into my voice. "The best is yet to come."

Her blue eyes looked at me. "I wish I could believe that. I'll be thirty-six soon. Over the hill as a movie actress. It makes me feel rather gloomy."

"Listen," I said, "good actresses get better with age. Look at Ingrid Bergman or Bette Davis. They've kept the exuberance of youth, and that keeps them young always. You have a plentiful supply."

"I hope you're right." She smiled and got up. We were both a little more sober now. "I'd better go. I'm leaving for California tomorrow and I've got to get my clothes ready." She picked up the manuscript. "I'll call you in the morning and let you know what I think of it."

The doorman flagged a cab for Marilyn and through the open window she kissed me softly and smiled. "Have a good sleep for me, Shutterbug," and she waved as the cab disappeared.

The doorman turned to me and said, "Wasn't that Marilyn Monroe?"

I nodded.

"God, she's a beaut," he said.

*Studio publicity still.*

*"Why must I always be the aggressor
with the men I want? Then as soon as
I get them, nothing ever works out. Is
this the cross I must bear for fame?
To be a love symbol, and not be loved?"*

*I* went to bed early that night, but I was restless and couldn't sleep. Marilyn didn't seem like her old self. She was quieter than usual, more solemn and introspective, and I wondered what was really bothering her. Loneliness? The fear that her beauty was slipping? Too many pills? Maybe all three—I just didn't know.

I lay there wide awake, remembering the things Marilyn had said to me, the way she looked, the sweet wistfulness in her eyes. My heart was heavy with compassion for her. She needed a man devoted solely to her, and to her life alone—one who would give her love, protection, and encouragement in endless doses. It would require the dedication and selflessness of a saint. DiMaggio had lasted only six months, and it had nearly cost Miller his sanity. Overwhelmed by futility, I finally fell asleep.

Ringing of the telephone awoke me. I looked groggily at my watch. It was 3:00 a.m. Hi, it's me, came Marilyn's voice. I've just read your book. I said, well, what's the verdict? The plot is great, but the characters are all wrong. I couldn't understand. How do you mean? You made a horror story out of your marriage. It should be a romantic adventure. I said, every word is the truth. That doesn't make it a good story. You've made your wife sound awful, and no one can sympathize with either of you. I asked her what I could do and she told me. I thanked her for the suggestions. You said once that imagination was the one quality all great writers had in common. Use it to create more believable characters. I thought about that. I think you're right. She laughed. When I complain about a lousy script, I wish I could get the studio bosses to say that. They don't believe a beautiful woman can think. That's the story of my life. But, I said, you're on top now. It should get easier. It doesn't. The pressure is always there. Every time I make a film I get sick. My body just won't handle the strain. The tension is unbelievable. Hey, she continued, your marriage sounds grim. I feel sorry for you. The island means so much to you. I can see it in your writing, the way you worship it. It's funny, I've fought to get a lot of men in my life, but I've never lost out to an island.

Three weeks later, Marilyn wrote to me from California.

When I came to Los Angeles, she promised, she would have the pool warmed up. She was afraid to use it until she learned to swim properly, and she asked "Shutterbug" to teach her. She reminded me that I'd started to once, patient with her in the desert heat, but all she did was flounder.

I constantly amazed her, she wrote; to her I was always so kind and even-tempered. Didn't I ever get angry or upset? She wondered if the peacefulness of my island life had made me unrufflable. She remembered that never once had I raised my voice or scolded her (how could I?) when she tried to drag me off to bed, even when she kept pestering me to marry her. She wouldn't again, she promised.

But, she wrote, it made her wonder—why must she always be the aggressor with the men she wanted? Then, as soon as she had them, nothing ever worked out. Was this the cross that she must bear for fame? To be a love symbol and not be loved? If so, she must never again look to marriage to fulfill all her needs. She would just have to satisfy her life with lovers and friends.

She asked how I was keeping, had I started rewriting the book. And, I was moved to read, she thought of me often, with much tenderness and love.

During this time Marilyn had taken up again with Sinatra and was seeing her Yankee Clipper (who occasionally slept over). She made a trip to Mexico to buy furniture for her house, which was now the center of her life. Carpenters were at work making alterations and she was studying garden books so that she could design her own garden. Meanwhile, Mrs. Murray had assumed the additional duties of companion, seamstress, and chauffeur. They went shopping together, discussed plans for an apartment over the two-car garage, and selected fruit trees at a nursery for the back yard.

Marilyn's new life alone had finally taken roots, and it was working. Her spirits were high, and she was enthusiastic about resuming her film career. "At last," she told me ecstatically on the phone, "I've got a place to entertain my friends. Just a few at a time, of course. I prefer not to mix them—like the Greensons and the Lawfords. I suppose it's selfish, but I don't like to share my friends with anybody."

Marilyn's social life had enlarged considerably. Through Sinatra she had met Peter Lawford and his wife, Dean Martin, and other members of the late Humphrey Bogart's Rat Pack. This clutch of stars were ardent Kennedy supporters, and the Lawford home in Santa Monica was considered by some as a West Coast extension of the White House.

Patricia Lawford was now Marilyn's closest friend, and Marilyn enjoyed her wit, sharp intelligence, and her sense of fun. "Even when I feel depressed," Marilyn remarked, "she can always make me laugh."

Through Pat it was inevitable that Marilyn would meet her famous brothers, President John Kennedy and Bobby Kennedy, the Attorney General, when they visited California. Marilyn admired the Kennedys greatly, not only for their political views, but because they were attractive and so young to be leaders of their country. She was drawn to success and excellence, to anyone who had accomplished much and from whom she could learn.

But the other side of Marilyn's dual Gemini nature sought such eminence to enhance her own image. In a sense she lived two lives at once, constantly keeping one or the other hidden from view. She was one moment ambitious actress, incorrigible romantic innocent the next. In the days ahead the conflict between these two selves—one a hardheaded realist, the other a wild-eyed believer that any dream could be fulfilled—would lead to her undoing.

In March, when Austin informed me he had heard from "reliable sources" that she had become involved with one of the Kennedys, I was concerned. Poor Marilyn. She was stepping into the murky world of politics, where often ambition and ruthlessness lie behind every action and every thought. The Kennedys were not only politicians, they were tough rich kids, Catholic, married, with children: an affair would have nowhere to go and could only

The Prince and the Showgirl.

hurt her. Lonely and starved for love, she was particularly vulnerable now.

Marilyn could not resist crowing about her conquests, and she phoned me with the news. "Hi, Shutterbug. It's me. I'm so excited," Marilyn said breathlessly. "I did it! I did it!"

"Did what?"

"I made it with the Prez."

"Who?"

She giggled. "You know, silly—President Kennedy."

"Oh," I said feebly.

"Hey, don't sound so excited. I've planned it for a long time. It's been a dream of mine."

"I'm sorry," I apologized, and asked with forced enthusiasm, "Where did this historic event take place?"

"Palm Springs. At Bing Crosby's desert house. Sometime between midnight and two A.M. We were walking together in the moonlight across the sand dunes. It happened so suddenly . . ." She sounded thrilled and happy.

"Listen," I said finally, "I hate to be a wet blanket. But JFK is a womanizer with the best track record in Washington. Be careful."

That seemed to amuse her and she laughed. "My record isn't so bad either. Maybe he'll rest on his laurels with what I've got to offer."

"Don't count on it, Sweetheart. Just play it cool."

*"Nobody objects to Goya's Naked Maja. Why should they object to my posing in the nude?"*

M arilyn began making her thirtieth film in April 1962; it was a comedy called *Something's Got to Give*, with Dean Martin. She was glad to be working again, even though she was not terribly enthused with either the story or the director, George Cukor, who she felt disliked her. Nor was she happy about receiving a salary of $100,000 while the studio was giving Elizabeth Taylor $1,000,000 a picture. She was pleased, however, with Nunnally Johnson's script, which she had personally okayed.

In Mexico she had picked up a virus that she couldn't shake. Suffering from anemia as well, Marilyn was often late and her missed days began to add up. Undaunted, she often worked with a high fever and severe headache. All the while Cukor kept changing the script, making it impossible for her to memorize her lines properly or formulate the character to be played. Daily changes were sent to her house on blue sheets of paper, until there was little left of the original script. Still, Marilyn reported on the set when she felt able, but now it was torture. It was as though the studio was out to destroy her.

Since Marilyn did not have script control written in her contract, she was

177

*1960.*

as helpless as she had been during *The Misfits* when Huston had overridden Miller and changed her part in a way she didn't like.

Marilyn was a serious performer, and the changes drove her to the brink of despondency. When she went home from the studio and attempted to study her lines for the next day's shooting, she felt it was useless. She washed down Valium with vodka. She was unable to relax without pills, or sleep without a handful of Nembutals. Alarmed, her analyst tried to reduce the barbiturates, but her internist, Dr. Hyman Engelberg, continued to prescribe them. I found this strange and I told Marilyn so. "I can't help it," she said. "They're both friends and are doing their best to help me. I trust them."

I was shocked. She seemed totally unaware of the danger. "Listen, Sweetheart. For your own good," I pleaded, "look for medical help elsewhere." And I recommended two doctors in the Los Angeles area whom I thought she might wish to consult.

"I'll think about it," she said.

The anxiety, the drug-induced sleep, and the savage hold of the virus weakened her more every day. After a month of shooting, Marilyn had reported in sick twelve days. Unpleasant rumors began to circulate, which made her furious. The reputation she had acquired for lateness and absence preyed heavily on her mind. Had she cried wolf once too often?

It rankled Marilyn that Elizabeth Taylor could be sick, delaying the production of *Cleopatra* at the cost of millions of dollars, without being accused of feigning illness. "Why can't they understand," she complained to me, "that I can be sick too?"

I sympathized with her, but I also knew that Fox was in serious financial trouble. Mindful of Elizabeth Taylor's huge cost to Fox on *Cleopatra*, the new studio boss, Peter Levathes, was seeking to tighten the pursestrings. He was hardly the man to pamper Marilyn. In fact, he ordered his producer, Henry Weinstein, to finish the picture without delay.

One Friday morning Marilyn played hookey and flew to New York, where she created a sensation on May 19 by singing "Happy Birthday" to President Kennedy in front of thousands in Madison Square Garden. She wore a skin-tight dress adorned with rhinestones and delivered the song in a sultry, intimate way no listener could ever forget, least of all Kennedy. Everybody loved it—everybody but 20th Century-Fox. Levathes was furious, even though the studio reaped millions of dollars of free publicity.

On Monday morning Marilyn was back at work. Though she knew she had stirred up a hornet's nest, she was full of smiles. Her wicked weekend had

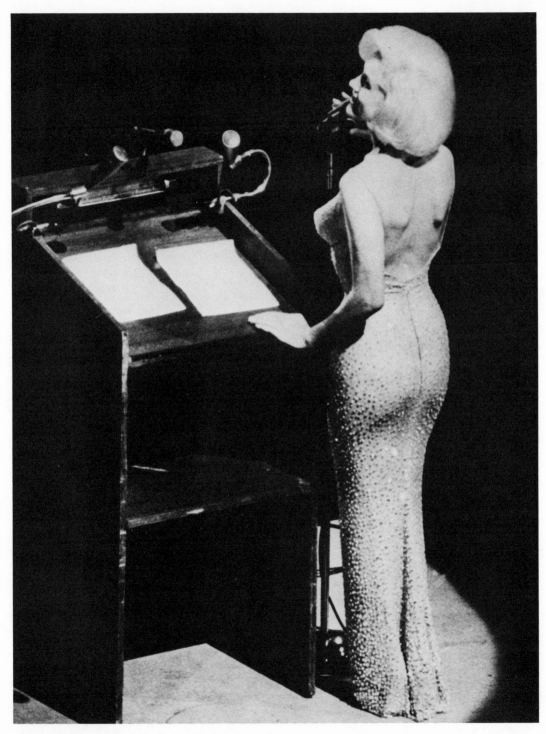

*Singing "Happy Birthday" to John F. Kennedy in
Madison Square Garden, May 19, 1962.*

done wonders for her spirit. She was ready and determined to give the command another jolt. The chance came on May 28, the Monday of her last week at Fox. The set had a swimming pool next to a plush two-story house. She was to do a nude swimming scene—wearing the customary flesh-colored bathing suit—to entice her ex-husband, played by Dean Martin, to go skinny-dipping with her.

Virus or not, Marilyn never looked more captivating or in trimmer shape as she plunged into the water. When the cameras began to roll, Marilyn slid off her suit and was dogpaddling—the only way she could swim—gleefully in the raw. Alert photographers Larry Schiller and Billy Woodfield snapped away as she cavorted in the pool like a playful child, jumping in and out numerous times to tease them, so they could capture her exquisite curves from every angle. In the most famous of these pictures she is peeking up over the edge of the pool with a devilish glint in her eyes. It is a look of triumph, as if all the insecurities and ugliness of Norma Jean's past have been exorcised, and at this moment emerges the free Marilyn.

Marilyn was proud of her body and loved to show it off. It was the one thing she always had confidence about. She felt her looks were her security. In four days she would be thirty-six, and she wanted to prove to herself and to the world that her figure, even at her age, was still the best feminine shape in existence. When the photographs were released, they did just that.

As Marilyn knew, the pictures could be worth a fortune—and they were. They appeared in over thirty countries; *Life* magazine paid $10,000 for the U.S. rights alone. Four days later, on June 1, when she was celebrating her birthday on the set, Larry Schiller asked what recompense she wanted for the shots. She thought a moment and responded, "A slide projector to show them on." The reply nearly brought tears to his eyes, for now he could afford to buy a house for his wife and family. Such generosity was typically Marilyn. She sent me a half dozen or so of the proofs with a note: "What do you think of these, Shutterbug?"

In an interview following the birthday party, my brother asked her about the "nude session" that had caused such an uproar. "What made you decide to swim in the raw?"

She replied, "Nobody objects to Goya's Naked Maja. Why should they object to my posing in the nude?"

Austin asked if this was the only reason, and she said, "The film is a dud. I just didn't care any longer." A good judge of scripts, Marilyn had seen that Cukor had changed Nunnally Johnson's work, which she had approved, and

180

this was her way of rebelling against the studio. She was tired of being treated like a commodity. "Besides," she said, grinning, "I want to be on all the magazine covers—not Liz Taylor."

Late that evening I finally reached Marilyn on the phone to wish her a happy birthday. She had just returned from Chavez Ravine, where she had made a benefit appearance. "I thought you were sick," I growled. "You shouldn't be out in that chilly night air."

"You're sweet, Shutterbug," she said. Her voice was slurred, undoubtedly from too much champagne. "But it was for charity. I couldn't go back on my promise."

"No, I'm angry."

"You shouldn't be. I did this for crippled children. You know how I love kids. I want to hug and kiss every one of them . . ." Her voice trailed off. Perhaps she was thinking of the child she always wanted—a baby girl, so that she could lavish on her all the love and attention that she had never had.

I asked her how she was feeling: "I've heard so many conflicting reports."

"Up and down. I can't rid of this awful virus. I've got a temperature all the time. Sometimes as much as a hundred and three. Then Dr. Engelberg discovered I have a sinus infection. Between the two, I feel so listless it makes me depressed."

"Poor Sweetheart. Have you someone there all the time?"

· "No. Mrs. Murray is only here during the day."

I didn't feel that in her condition she should be by herself, and I asked, "Why doesn't she live with you?"

"I need time alone to recharge myself. That's what I tell everybody. But the truth is, how can you have any fun with servants always around?" She giggled. "After all, Joe sleeps over now and then and he hates to be seen by anyone."

I laughed. She sounded in good spirits. Marilyn enjoyed being secretive. She always kept a wall of privacy around herself. One thing she never did was divulge her intimate life or private thoughts to servants or associates, not even to Natasha Lytess, with whom she lived for a while. Miss Lytess recalled later, "I dared not ask her the simplest questions about her life. Even an inquiry as to where she might be going on a certain evening would be regarded as unpardonable prying."

"How is Mrs. Murray working out?"

"To be honest, I really don't feel comfortable with her," Marilyn said.

"She discourages my friends from coming to see me. Poor Ralph Roberts, my masseur, gets the dirtiest looks. He just hates to come here anymore. Besides, I don't trust her. I think she tells Dr. Greenson everything. Oh, well, I've got too much to do to worry."

I asked, "How often do you see Dr. Greenson?"

"Almost every day. And sometimes Dr. Engelberg, too. He gives me shots for my anemia." I didn't want to bring up again the touchy subject of her changing doctors. This was her birthday, no time to upset her.

"It's a wonder you're still on your feet."

Her voice was strained. "I haven't any choice," she said. "I've got to finish the film. Then I won't have to see that horrible studio again."

"Surely they know how sick you are," I said with concern.

"They don't give a damn. I hate Weinstein and the whole fucking lot. I go to work when I'm able to," she began to sob, "but so much of the time I can't . . . I just can't . . ."

*"I feel I'm just beginning. I want to
do all kinds of films—comedy,
romance, tragedy. After all, without
a challenge what is there to life?"*

*F*or several days now rain has confined guests to their cottages,
and the air has the smell of evergreens and smoke. In the store,
there's been a run on cocoa, marshmallows, magazines, pop, and post-
cards. The drizzle doesn't seem to bother anyone except the Hoveys,
a Santa Barbara couple. The first symptoms appeared Wednesday when
Mr. Hovey sputtered, "Does it always rain here, Mr. Conover?"

*June 8.* The news came over the radio today that Fox fired Marilyn.
I wonder how she's taking it.

Apparently Marilyn was more angered than stunned by the blow. She
knew any studio would jump at the chance to have her. The main thing that
made her unhappy was that others on the set—grip men and gaffers and
stagehands, all of whom she considered her friends—had lost their jobs, and
she wired them an apology, that she was deeply sorry. Dean Martin's ulti-
matum to the studio, "No Marilyn, no Dino," cheered her immeasurably
and helped offset the uncomplimentary things appearing in the press about
her.

185

My radiotelephone was on the blink at the time. But once fixed, it wasn't long before she phoned to tell me the news herself.

I made very light of her firing. "Consider it an unexpected holiday, Sweetheart. You've won all your studio battles. You'll win this one. They'll be at your doorstep crawling on their knees."

"Hey, you really think so?"

"Yes, really," I said confidently. "The top brass is too insulated from the public. The people made you a star long before the studio was aware of it. How do I know? Because you were a box-office sensation without having made a top film." I went on, "Fox has terribly underestimated your huge following. Millions of devoted fans who feel for you and believe in you. They'll soon recognize their mistake. That's why you'll be reinstated. Meanwhile, forget the film, keep busy and have fun. Think only how you can enlarge yourself—or advance your career."

"You mean do more publicity photographs?"

"Yes. All kinds. Crash the ladies' magazines, but stay out of *Playboy*. Also, do more nudes like the ones you sent. They're terrific."

I knew her impulse to show off her body was irresistible to her, and that it would boost her morale to have an occasion to do it. She was never more relaxed and confident than before the still camera. Except, perhaps, standing naked before a full-length mirror—which she did—preening and admiring herself in a sort of trance of dreamy amazement. She was narcissist in the purest sense; for her, nudity was akin to a state of innocence. There was no embarrassment, no qualms about being seen naked by masses of people. In fact, it made her feel triumphant, happy, and secure. She felt people loved her, and to be surrounded by love and affection was what she sought most from life.

"You know something, Sweetheart?" I said, glancing at her photographs as we talked.

"No, what?"

"You grow more beautiful with age."

"Hey, thanks."

I knew that during the last year Marilyn's addiction to barbiturates had grown considerably. They threatened her health and ability to work. Now with no one like Miller around to restrain her intake, I was worried. "Just remember, Sweetheart," I said, trying not to sound preachy, "you have a very special talent. A unique talent never before seen on the screen. Think of it as a special gift. Every time you take too many pills or drink too heavily, you are destroying this gift. Honor it and it will always honor you."

"Hey," came her breathless voice. "You almost make me believe I am something special."

"You are, Sweetheart."

"But I've got so many hang-ups—so many fears. I hope I won't ever disappoint you."

"You won't."

"You seem so sure. How do you know?"

I laughed. "You haven't got this far on looks alone. It takes a shrewd and determined mind—plus lots of guts."

"Oh, Shutterbug. You're a doll."

"Don't try to flatter me. I'll take back everything I said."

"You shouldn't be so modest. I wouldn't be where I am today without you."

"Nonsense. Somebody else would have come along."

Spunk and resiliency were the basic elements of her being, and Marilyn could always count on them. They had taken her from a nobody to a somebody. They would see her through now.

All through June, Marilyn involved herself in a whirlwind of activity that left her little time for introspection. She posed for *Vogue, Cosmopolitan,* and *Life,* each session requiring hours of makeup and hairstyling. In a sudden grip of stage fever, she flew to New York, where the Strasbergs gave her the role of Blanche Du Bois in *Streetcar,* and she stunned the members of the Actors Studio with a brilliant performance.

Like a true Gemini, she would meet herself coming and going, jetting back again to her Brentwood hacienda, her unused swimming pool, and her analyst, Dr. Ralph Greenson. She considered a backlog of film and TV offers, granted a lengthy interview to Richard Meryman for *Life,* and took up again with Sinatra, DiMaggio, and the Lawfords.

She was entering the last two weeks of her life.

Meanwhile, as I'd predicted, Fox executives were knocking on her door, wooing her back into the fold, and Marilyn's spirits had never been higher. As much as she disliked the mutilated script of *Something's Got to Give,* she agreed to finish the picture because of Dean Martin's loyalty; she wasn't about to let him down. The film would resume when Martin returned in September from a night club engagement in Las Vegas.

Her career and future were now in hand, and she had more time to fill,

*1955.*

fighting the ever advancing spectre of loneliness. She was said to spend hours on the telephone. Austin told me she was often at the Lawfords, where she met Bobby Kennedy every time he flew to the Coast; his trips grew increasingly frequent. Many a night when she was sexually restive and unable to sleep, she called Ralph Roberts, her faithful masseur, to come to the house to give her a massage. "This is a lot better than pills," she told him. He found her slimmer and in better health than she'd been in a long time. She also told him about the man in her life, but he already knew: "All Hollywood is talking of nothing else." The rumors of a serious involvement were far too persistent for there not to be a relationship of some kind. Poor Marilyn, I thought, if the rumors were true.

It was late July. I hadn't heard from her in some time, and I knew the reason. Deeply concerned, I had to know the truth. When I finally reached Marilyn on the phone, she seemed both agitated and depressed. "What's wrong?" I asked, frankly worried now. "You don't sound like your bubbly self."

She hesitated. "I suppose you know. I mean, about Bobby and me?"

"Yes."

"Well, if you're going to tell me 'I told you so,' please don't. I'm in a foul mood. I don't think I could take it."

"I won't—I promise. Go ahead, Sweetheart. Tell me everything."

"Bobby said he loved me and asked me to marry him when he got a divorce. Then the bastard ran out on me. I can't get hold of him at the Justice Department, or anywhere. He just won't return my calls." She sounded terribly hurt and bitter by the rejection, and I wondered what I could say.

"Maybe he's busy," I tried lamely. "On government business somewhere."

"No." She paused. "I told him I was pregnant."

"Are you?"

"I was," she admitted. "But I had it taken care of right away. It was another tubular pregnancy."

"Does anyone else know?"

"No. I haven't told anybody. Not even Joe. He's so mad at me now over this whole thing he hardly speaks to me. I've tried to write him—but I can't get the words down I want to say. I don't want to lose his friendship. It means too much to me."

What she wanted to tell Joe, Marilyn said, was that if she could make him happy, she would be accomplishing the most marvelous thing she could think of—making one person completely happy. Joe's happiness, to put it simply, was Marilyn's happiness. (The letter was finally written but never sent. It was found in her desk after her death.)

I said emphatically, "It's best not to tell anyone about Bobby."

"Well," she suddenly turned obstinate, "if he keeps on avoiding me, I'm going to call a press conference. Spill everything. I'll really make that bastard squirm."

I told her that wouldn't be a wise thing to do. Not only would it be dangerous, but she'd be hurting herself. Vindictiveness wasn't the image the public held of her, and it wasn't part of her nature.

"I'm sorry." She softened. "Maybe you're right. But I still think I deserve an explanation or an apology."

I advised her to forget the whole matter, to chalk the affair up to experience and get on with her life. "It's only by thinking positive," I said, "that good things can happen."

"But I don't understand," she went on. "I told him I'd get an abortion. Why does he keep avoiding me?"

I thought for a moment. "Maybe he suddenly found himself in a dangerous situation. You know—a compromising one."

"How do you mean?"

"Bobby's got more enemies than anyone else in Washington. Powerful ones, like Hoffa. I'm sure they'd like to get something on him. Wouldn't you think?"

"Hey—shh . . . don't say anything more. I'll call you right back." She hung up.

Fifteen minutes later, the radio operator called Wallace Island. It was Marilyn. "Sorry. Things just made sense. I think my phone is bugged, so I'm at a pay phone. I've been hearing a lot of clicks and strange sounds on the line lately. Do you suppose this has anything to do with what we were talking about?"

"Undoubtedly. Unless it's Bobby checking up on you."

"I don't think so. He didn't seem the jealous type. In fact, he was kinda nice really." She giggled and began to sound more cheerful. "Very sweet, tender, thoughtful—and a marvelous lover."

I ignored this. "When did you first notice your phone was tapped?"

"About three weeks ago, I think."

"Did you tell Bobby about it?" I asked.

"Yes, the last time I saw him."

"What did he say?"

"That I was imagining things. And to forget it."

190

I thought that very odd. "You mean, he didn't seem upset, or say anything about it?"

"No. But now that I think of it, he did say he had to leave sooner than he expected. 'Official business.' "

The picture was becoming clearer. He undoubtedly wanted to make his own investigation before the culprits were scared away. "Did Bobby ever spend the night at your place?"

"No. He came to the house only once. During the day and just for a short time. He always insisted that I meet him at the Lawfords. He said he felt safer there."

"Does that tell you something?"

"Uh huh. Somebody has been using me to put the finger on him?"

"Right. Everytime he sees you secretly, he leaves himself open to blackmail."

"You really think so?" She sounded frightened now.

"Absolutely." Bobby Kennedy had said more than once that he would put Jimmy Hoffa in jail no matter what it took. Hoffa, with all his gangster connections, was not a man to be threatened. Since the Kennedy family was wealthy and could not be bought, only one defense existed—blackmail.

"How awful," Marilyn breathed when I laid this out to her. "I didn't realize I'd be getting involved in anything like this."

I didn't want to scare her—but she was scaring me. Not only did she suspect her phone was bugged, she told me her files had been broken into and searched. I didn't want her to get mixed up in this dangerous situation. "Now do you see," I said sternly, "how important it is to forget the whole idea of exposing Bobby? You might be playing right into the hands of the hoods bugging your line who are out after him. He's shunning you for good reason—his political life."

Marilyn was silent for a moment. "I can't believe that Bobby didn't mean all those promises he made me."

"He got what he wanted, I believe. Didn't he?"

"Yeah, the bastard. I've never known anyone so two-faced. He could at least have said, 'Thanks. I had a grand time. Goodbye.' Instead of running out on me."

When I asked Marilyn if she had spoken about denouncing Bobby to anyone else, she said, "Yes, with a close friend." She didn't name the friend, and I didn't ask who it was.

"What did he advise?"

"Same thing as you." She chuckled. "Forget him."

After that, Marilyn talked about furnishing her house. "The rooms look so bare," she said. "I can't wait until the handmade rugs and the tables and chairs arrive from Mexico. The house will be so pretty and cozy I'll never want to leave it."

She spoke enthusiastically about her future plans. The possible night club engagement in Las Vegas. Renovating her guest house. Drawing up a new will. The resumption of *Something's Got to Give* in September. A discussion with movie producer Arthur Jacobs about the possibility of making *What a Way to Go*. And in the not too distant future, flying to New York to visit the Strasbergs.

We talked about the possibilities that lay ahead for her when her contract ended at Fox. To become a serious actress was very much on her mind. "I feel I'm just beginning," she said. "I want to do all kinds of films—comedy tragedy, romance. After all, without a challenge what is there to life?" Her voice was filled with the spirit of vitality that on the screen so radiantly illuminated her face.

That's my Marilyn, I thought, and I grinned.

She was happy and excited about the future. I asked her, "Have you read Somerset Maugham's *Of Human Bondage?*"

"I don't think so. Why?"

"There's a great dramatic part in it for you. The role of Mildred. It launched Bette Davis's career and made her a star almost overnight. You could do even better."

"Really?" She sounded pleased.

"Sure," I told her. "Bette Davis portrayed only the harsh side of Mildred, the seamy and obviously dramatic. You would be capable of showing both sides of her nature. The sweet as well as the nasty."

"Oh, Shutterbug—you believe in me so much, it scares me. Really."

"Why shouldn't I? You've got the ability. The desire. Everything . . ."

"Except confidence," she breathed softly.

I knew this was true, but how do you go about giving another person *self-*confidence? "Listen," I said firmly. "Repeat after me: I'm going to be the best damned actress Hollywood has ever seen."

"Okay." Marilyn repeated the words.

"Again."

And she did, laughing.

I told her to say those words to herself every night before she went to sleep. She said that she would.

"Now do me a favor."

"Anything—"

"I'd like an invite when you collect your first Oscar."

"It's a deal." She giggled.

That was our last conversation. Ten days later my Marilyn was dead.

## EPILOGUE

*"Goodbye Norma Jean. Au revoir*
*Marilyn. When you happen on Bobby*
*and Jack, give the wink. And if there's*
*a wish, pay your visit to Mr. Dickens.*
*For he, like many another literary man,*
*is bound to adore you, fatherless child."*
*Norman Mailer, Marilyn*

*A*t first, like everybody else, I accepted the coroner's verdict: "probable suicide." All of the known facts, at that time, pointed to an overdose of barbiturates. But over the years that followed a mass of evidence has been uncovered that unquestionably indicates that Marilyn's death was murder disguised as suicide. No one close to Marilyn, including myself, really believed that she had taken her own life. Despite her periods of instability—who has not had them?—Marilyn had too much to look forward to, too much to live for. And she knew it. This is a view shared by Eunice Murray, her housekeeper and the last person known to see Marilyn alive.

To Marilyn's old friend, Robert Slatzer, author of *The Life and Curious Death of Marilyn Monroe*, we owe credit for bringing to light the overwhelming evidence of murder. And, in my small way, I wish to substantiate his findings. The calls we *both* received from Marilyn shortly before her death were from a pay phone because she was afraid and didn't dare talk on her own phone. She told both Slatzer and me that she couldn't understand why her phone was bugged, why her files had been ransacked.

I was sure at the time, and told her so, that she was caught up in a vicious battle between union leader Jimmy Hoffa and Bobby Kennedy, then Attorney General, and advised her most emphatically not to play the scorned woman with Bobby and, above all, not to try to expose their affair to the press. It was much too dangerous. A few days later, Marilyn was dead.

Marilyn did not stretch out to die on her crumpled sheet from taking a fatal overdose of Nembutals. No trace of drugs was found in her stomach, only in the liver and blood. Former police sergeant Jack Clemmons, the first officer on the scene, told Slatzer he believes Marilyn was murdered by someone she knew and trusted, who administered the drug by suppository or injection into the bloodstream. He was shocked to high heaven by the official conclusion of suicide. Clemmons also stated that the original homicide reports were changed, evidence disappeared, and Los Angeles police chief Bill Parker (who had been promised J. Edgar Hoover's job) rushed to Washington to see Bobby Kennedy.

But this isn't the only evidence of foul play.

Breaking his silence on the case for the first time in seventeen years, former deputy coroner Lionel Grandison declared, "It was obviously death at the hands of another (*Los Angeles Sunday Mirror*, April 22, 1979). He asserted that, in spite of his reluctance, his superiors had forced him to sign the death certificate of the thirty-six-year-old movie star, which stated that on August 5, 1962, she had taken a fatal overdose of forty-seven Nembutals. He now admits that the investigation was a farce.

I think it's high time for the Los Angeles authorities to get off their butts and remove the cloak of mystery that hangs so shamefully around Marilyn's death. It is almost a certainty that she died as the direct result of her entanglement with Bobby and Jack Kennedy. How and by whom her life was ended is not clear, because of the wholesale suppression of evidence by the Los Angeles coroner's office and the police department, and the many contradictory statements of witnesses.

But homicide has no statute of limitations. Nearly all the people who were with Marilyn or who spoke with her during her last days—and who could point to her killers—are still alive (her analyst, Dr. Greenson, died in 1979). The case demands a new investigation. I hope and pray, along with millions of others, that the present district attorney is a man of honor and justice, and will soon order a complete re-examination of the case. These are among the questions that deserve to be answered:

Did Chief of Police William H. Parker confiscate Marilyn's phone records— and, if so, why?

Why did Dr. Ralph Greenson and Dr. Hyman Engelberg take as long as they did to notify the police?

Why was Sergeant Jack Clemmons, a highly respected veteran police officer, dropped from the force a short time later, after he maintained that Marilyn's death was an "out and out case of murder"?

Why and at whose urging did Mrs. Murray and Pat Newcomb, Marilyn's press secretary, make lengthy trips abroad after Marilyn's death?

Did Dr. Thomas Noguchi, the deputy medical examiner, fail to perform a proper autopsy?

Why was Coroner Lionel Grandison forced to sign a fraudulent death certificate?

Why has Marilyn's death file in the Hall of Records been unavailable to investigators?

*Who, after all, was responsible for Marilyn's death?*

We, the people, are entitled to know the truth. We owe it to Marilyn, who gave us so much and who still continues to live in our hearts as well as in her films. "She died before she had achieved anything like her full potential," remarked Edward Wagenknecht in his thoughtful book, *Marilyn Monroe: A Composite View.* "And very often the material she had to work with was trash, but this made no particular difference, for she was one of those curious persons who always make you feel that they themselves are so much more important than anything they do."

Shortly before her death, in the interview with Richard Meryman that appeared in *Life,* she declared, "If I am a star, the people made me a star— no studio, no person, but the people did." This was true, of course. The public made Marilyn a star long before she was given featured billing in a top film. The studio bosses were as nearsighted and as callous as Marilyn was devoid of rancor or guile. This was a woman who spoke of her former husbands as "two of the nicest men I had met up to that time," adding that she "was lucky enough to marry them."

Her generosity of spirit was triumphant to the end. I have benefited greatly by it, for without her criticism of my first manuscript I would never have become a published writer. Thanks to Marilyn's insights, *Once Upon an Island* was not only published, it sold well in nine languages and gave me the encouragement in the midstream of life to change careers.

I like to think that the Marilyn I knew nobody else knew, at least not in the same way. Over the years, our vastly different lives touched each other at infrequent intervals, yet our close relationship prospered despite time and distance and strengthened and stimulated each of us. Our worlds were poles apart: I needed only to stand a few minutes at Hollywood and Vine to be recharged for a full year, ready to return to the beauty and simplicity of island life. It made me wonder if success isn't really the freedom to live the life you want.

As my island was everything I wanted in life, Marilyn was everything I wanted a girl to be: beautiful, witty, talented, creative, warm, understanding, and eminently cuddleable. When the opportunity arose—and there were many—I found myself touching her. But no matter what my heart said, I knew we could never have shared our lives.

It is difficult to be objective about someone you love, and still more difficult if you are responsible for bringing that person to the attention of the world. But I believe that all through her life Marilyn missed desperately the safe and quiet anchorage of a family. I became to her the father she had never had—and teacher, lover, psychiatrist, confidant, marriage counselor, and business adviser. I never thought of her as a sex goddess or a movie queen. She was a woman, sometimes frightened, often confused; a woman who in many ways was still a child, who with courage was learning to reach out and grow, to mature as an individual and in her art. I knew she had both the drive and the talent to become a great actress. There was no doubt in my mind—or in Lee Strasberg's—about that. But when I thought of her vulnerability, I was always inclined to say a prayer.

"Heart" is the word that best describes Marilyn. She was all heart, much too sensitive and kind for her own good. As a result, she often depended on the wrong kind of people and took a lot of bad advice. She was secretive and purposely kept her friends apart so they wouldn't talk to each other and compare notes, a stratagem she adopted because of her mistrust and insecurity. She did not altogether trust even the psychiatrists whom she frequented. She could not really bare her soul to them. When a session got to the nitty-gritty, she'd nearly always fantasize. I scolded her about this, but she laughed that celebrated little-girl laugh of hers and said, "Hey, I'm paying the shot. Why shouldn't I say what I damn well please?" On another occasion Marilyn complained, "Analysts only tell you what you want to hear. What's the good of that?" Yet she went on seeing them. Towards the last, they served merely to push back the loneliness.

With me, however, I felt Marilyn could always speak her mind. Removed from the Hollywood scene and with no axe to grind, I could view events and circumstances in her life dispassionately. Yet this wasn't always easy. In both her career and her marriages she lived from crisis to crisis. I never knew when I would hear that familiar greeting, "Hi! It's me, Shutterbug," come over the airwaves. Usually her calls to me came late at night and she'd pour out her problems, her voice often choked with tears. Many times they were not as serious as she believed, and frequently we could resolve them by talking them out. I would weigh the pros and cons of each step that she could take and then let her come to her own decision, offering an opinion only when urged to. I wanted to build Marilyn's confidence in her own judgment, which as a rule was very sound.

When several weeks went by without a call from Marilyn, I knew all was going well. Other times, she'd call just to have somebody to talk to, or when she was unable to sleep, and we'd chat for hours about the current man in her life, the film she was making, her grievances with Fox. She was one of the few people who can be both articulate and funny at three A.M. "Hey, I've got a question," she said in her silky voice late one night.

"Yes," I mumbled sleepily.

"What makes a man smoke after he makes love?"

"I dunno."

She giggled. "Because he can't do anything else."

Marilyn was often difficult to understand because her life was so full of paradoxes. In Hollywood, where ego is God, she suffered from an inferiority complex. The making of movies frightened her. She struggled for perfection in her career—and often obtained it—yet was continually dissatisfied with her performance. She had to have that one more take. She was the most loved of all movie stars, and the most abused by the film industry; the most adored woman of her time, and the loneliest of people. At her death, Marilyn was undoubtedly the most desired woman in the world, and she spent her last Saturday night alone.

Without a mate who could ease the burden of her tortured spirit, Marilyn used the phone as her last weapon against loneliness. It was a cruel stroke of fate that she would die with this instrument in her hand. Help is the one thing every human being needs. Marilyn, perhaps, of all people needed it the most.

In retrospect, it seems to me that the triumph and the tragedy of her life are more fascinating than any film she ever made. I feel sometimes humble that, on the periphery of Marilyn's life, I was part of it—yet I am never free of the feeling of guilt that I should have done more, that if I had she still might be alive.